The BIG LITTLE BOOK® Price Guide

James Stuart Thomas

Big Little Book® is a registered trademark of Western Publishing Company, Inc.

Cover Design: Jerry Alingh

Library of Congress
Catalog Card Number 82-050484

ISBN 0-87069-414-6

10 9 8 7 6 5 4 3 2 1

Copyright © 1983
James Stuart Thomas

All rights reserved. No part of this publication may be reproduced, stored in a retrieval system, or transmitted in any form or by any means, electronic, mechanical, photocopying, recording or otherwise, without prior permission of the copyright owner or the publisher.

Published by

Wallace-Homestead Book Company
1912 Grand Avenue
Des Moines, Iowa 50305

To my family

Acknowledgments

I would like to thank the following for their expertise and their advice:
  Dr. Rick Breitenfeld
  Dr. Milton C. Cummings, Jr.
  William R. Evans
  M.C. Hill
  H.I. Stroth of Studio VII in Lexington, Kentucky
  Western Publishing Company, Inc.
I would also like to thank my family and friends for their support.

Preface

The *Big Little Book® Price Guide* provides market information for a rapidly growing branch of comics collecting. This guide includes every element that contributes to the value of a book. Prices quoted herein reflect current market values. Months of research went into price comparisons to insure accuracy. Prices are to be used as estimates of what a collector might expect to pay. Dealers, who carry the burden of overhead, usually will pay from 25 to 80 percent of these prices, depending on the desirability of the book.

Publishers of Big Little Books® listed in this guide are arranged as follows: the two most significant companies with whom most collectors associate Big Little Books® are placed in order of importance—Whitman first, followed by Saalfield. The remaining publishers are listed alphabetically according to their company name, not their book series logo. Wherever possible, series numbers, authors, artists, and dates, as well as many other items of market interest, are included. Because the goal of this publication is to supply complete, correct information, I urgently request the reader to notify me of all omissions or errors. Contributions to any future editions will be acknowledged, but should be accompanied by photostatic copies or some other form of documentation wherever possible.

Contents

Acknowledgments 4
Preface 5
Introduction 9
   Giveaways, Miniatures, and Other Variants 11
   Fast Action® and Dime Action® Books 12

The Big Little Book® Market 13
   Determinants of Value 13
   How to Store Your Big Little Books® 17
   Terminology 18

Whitman Publishing Company 19
   Big Little® and Better Little® Books (1932-1949) 20
   New Better Little® Books (1949-1950) 89
   Big Little Book TV Series® (1958) 90
   A Big Little Book® (1967-1969, 1973-present) 91
   Variant Big Little Books® (1933-1943) 103

Saalfield Publishing Company 131
   Little Big Books® (1934-1938) 132
   Jumbo Books® (1938-1940) 142

Dean and Son, Ltd. 146
Engel-Van Wiseman, Inc. 147
Fawcett Publications, Inc. 149
Golden Press Publishing Company
 (Western Publishing) 149
Goldsmith Publishing Company 150
Lynn Publishing Company, Inc. 150
McLoughlin Brothers
 Publishing Company 152
Ottenheimer Publishers, Inc. 152
Playmore Incorporated 153
Samuel Lowe Company 154
 The Swap-It® Books 154
 Smokey Joe of the Glendale Riders® 156
Wehrle, Joe, Jr. 157
World Syndicate Publishing Company 157

Introduction

Big Little Books® (BLBs) had their roots in children's books of the early 1900s. The Whitman Publishing Company, the originator of BLBs, ran a line of series books in the 1920s. These included the Fairy Tale, Sunny Hour, Friendly Animal, Forest Friends, Campfire Girl, Sleepy Road, and Daddy Duck series. The latter series included the *Mother Goose Paint and Drawing Book,* a possible source for the highly sought Big Little Book 725. One of these early series most directly influenced the modern BLB—the Boy Adventure series, which produced titles like *Ted Marsh* and *Buffalo Bill and the Pony Express,* later to appear as regular BLBs.

The first Big Little Book® bearing that logo was *The Adventures of Dick Tracy* (707), published by Whitman. The books came into full production in 1933. These small, fat, and square "board covered books," as they were called, served as vehicles for newspaper comic strip reprints and condensed movie stories. The first BLBs measured $4\frac{1}{4}$ x 4 x $1\frac{3}{8}$ inches and had 320 pages. Those containing movie adaptations measured $3\frac{5}{8}$ x $4\frac{1}{4}$ x $1\frac{1}{4}$ inches and had only 240 pages with photos, instead of drawings, opposite the text. Since then, many variations in size and page counts have been produced, sometimes within a single title.

The World Syndicate Publishing Company followed Whitman's lead, putting out the Highlights of History® series by J. Carroll Mansfield in 1933. These were all-picture BLBs, reprinted from Mansfield's comic strip of the same name. Two versions of these books exist—one with a four-color illustrated cover like traditional BLBs, and another with a thread-sewn plain clothlike cover in red, white, blue or black, with an imprinted title and, sometimes, a simple line drawing of the illustrated cover. The series folded in 1934.

Whitman's largest competitor, the Saalfield Publishing Company, began making their version of Big Little Books®—Little Big Books®—in 1934. Possibly their greatest contribution to the BLB field was their movie stories and biographies. Saalfield introduced Elzie C. Segar's Popeye to the BLB world as well. Little Big Books® were not as sturdy as Big Little Books®, resulting in many today with no spines or covers. In 1939, Saalfield changed the name of their BLBs to Jumbo Books,® a title that lasted until 1940 when the series ended.

The Five Star Library® also appeared in 1934. The books in this series, published by the Engel-Van Wiseman Publishing Company, were thinner and taller than traditional BLBs, and contained movie stories in all but one title. Perhaps their most notable contribution was their use of big name stars, or those that went on to become big stars. Among those names were John Wayne, Katherine Hepburn, Douglas Fairbanks, a very young Alan Hale, and even Franklin Roosevelt. The series ended in 1935.

Other publishers who had their own versions of Big Little Books® included the Lynn Publishing Company, which began in 1935 and ended in 1936, and the Goldsmith Publishing Company, whose BLBs of 1934-1935 introduced the artwork of Henry Vallely, an artist who later went to Whitman and turned out some of the finest Big Little Books® of all time.

Not all Big Little Books® had pictures opposite the text. There were many BLBs, especially the early or more literary ones, that had more text than drawings. The most common examples are the Zane Grey and condensed novel titles. At the other extreme, the all-picture and tall comic series had no text, except for word balloons in the comic story itself.

Throughout the 1930s, Whitman experimented with different formats and title variations. There were Big Big Books,® Penny Books,® Big Little Nickel Books,® Wee Little Books,® Top Line Comics,® All Pictures Comics,® and The Feature Movie Books.® In 1938, Whitman changed the name of their books to The Better Little Books® and reduced the number of pages. During the title changeover, ten books known as transition books were published with logo alterations—a black overprint of the round trademark logo. Six titles appear with both the solid black logo and the Big Little Book® logo, and one title, *Mickey Mouse in the Race for Riches,* 1476, was published in three versions: with the black overprint; with the Big Little Book® logo; and with the Better Little Book® logo. Transition books with the Big Little Book® logo are rare.

BLBs carried the Better Little Book® logo until mid-1949, when the name was changed to New Better Little Books.® These books had a narrower and thinner format. Some were published with black and white illustrations, and some carried monocolored pages—either red, blue, or green. This series lasted until mid-1950. In 1958, the format was changed again, this time to a slightly larger hardback design with laminated covers and uninteresting illustrations, again in monocolor, but alternated with some pages one color, other pages another. These were called The Big Little Book TV Series,® as they were based on popular television shows. Production stopped after only six titles.

From 1959 to the mid-1960s, Big Little Books® were replaced by Whitman Big Book Adventures® (based on movies and television series), Whitman Classics® (abridged versions of such titles as *Huckleberry Finn* and *Robinson Crusoe)* and Whitman Tween-Age Books.®

Then in 1967, BLBs were brought back with *Dick Tracy Encounters Facey* under a new series called A Big Little Book.® These books were similar to the Better Little Books,® however, they were thinner and contained full four-color drawings. This new series produced books based on television shows, cartoons, comic strips, and even a toy—Major Matt Mason. This group of BLBs consists of two sets: the 2000 series (1967-1969), and a set of reprint and modern stories—the 5700 series (1973-present). The first series, a hardcover set, sells better than the latter.

Interestingly, Whitman produced another set of BLBs under the publishing name, Golden Press. This series, called A Golden Star Book® (listed in this guide under Golden Press), had the same dimensions as the 2000 series of A

Better Little Books,® yet were considered classier in text and picture content, having illustrations instead of line drawings. These books were originally published in Paris, France, by Deux Coqs d'Or in 1966. These books were written and illustrated by French artists, for the most part, and have a table of contents at the back of the book in traditional French style.

Giveaways, Miniatures, and Other Variants

In 1933, Whitman began producing a series of softbound premiums to be given away by various companies as promotional items. The most common of these were the Cocomalt giveaways. These books were approximately the same height and width of a regular BLB, but had as many as 100 fewer pages. In the case of the Cocomalt books, the premiums had an ad for Cocomalt food drink on the back cover, on the inside front and back covers, and on the last page of the story. Other companies, like Phillips Dental Magnesia and Amoco Gas, also distributed these books.

In 1935, Whitman began experimenting with other types of premium BLBs. Three sets were distributed to various businesses through agencies like Perkins and Karmetz — two companies responsible for distributing most of these new, smaller giveaways. Among these sets were giveaways associated with the Kool-Aid/Lemix-Korlix Company, Kay Kamen and Sears Department Stores, Pan-Am Gas, and Macy's. Other premium BLBs of this type exist without corporation advertisements on the back cover. These books were intended for local distribution. The back cover was left blank so that shoe stores, grocery stores, and clothing stores could furnish their own stamps, although some of these businesses neglected to do so. Still another set exists that bears no advertisement and includes some of the rarer Tarzan titles. These were usually miniatures with dimensions between $3\frac{1}{2}$ x $3\frac{1}{2}$ inches and $3\frac{1}{2}$ x $5\frac{5}{8}$ inches and page counts from 48 to 144 pages.

One of the more popular sets of Big Little Book® premiums is the Tarzan Cup-Lid series distributed by the Lily-Tulip Corporation to promote their Tarzan Ice Cream product. These books were given out in exchange for twelve Tarzan Ice Cream cup lids. These giveaways are hard to find in nice condition for two reasons: first, they were cheaply bound with a soft cover and staples; second, the back cover served as a grand prize coupon page. The reader could send this coupon and twenty Tarzan lids (with the backs of five other books in the set) and get one of thirteen full-length Tarzan novels free. The first set of Tarzan cup-lid premiums contained twelve numbered titles, copyrighted 1934 and 1936. Between these dates, in 1935, another set was made containing six unnumbered titles. Both the numbered and unnumbered sets are identical in size and format, except the first set has 128 pages, while the second set has 144.

Another set of ice-cream giveaways was made in 1938. Buddy Books®, as they are called, were given away when twelve Buddy Book coupons were redeemed. The coupons were given with each purchase of an ice-cream cone. Buddy Books® are similar to Tarzan cup-lid books. However, the grand prize coupons were printed on the last page of the book instead of on the back cover.

Whitman published several other types of Big Little Books® with various series names. In 1934, these three variant formats were produced: Wee Little Books,® Big Big Books,® and Famous Comics.® The first consisted of six sets of six books each. Each set was devoted to one character or theme and came in library-style half-boxes. The Wee Little Books® were 3½ x 3⅝ x ⅛ inches and had 40 pages, with a soft cover glued to the book. Big Big Books® were large hardback BLBs that sold for twenty-five cents. Because of their large, awkward size, many of these books suffered damage, particularly to the spine. They measured 7¼ x 9½ x 1¼ inches and had 320 pages. Not many of these books were purchased because of their high price, and they were discontinued in 1938. Famous Comics,® like the Wee Little Books,® also came in a box. The set contained three books, 3½ x 8½ x ¼ inches with 96 pages each, and each book was made up of reprinted comic strips of various characters.

In 1935, four sets of boxed miniature BLBs known as Top-Line Comics® appeared. There were three books to a box with each book having 160 pages. In 1937, Nickel Books® were published. These were flat, 64-page storybooks that sometimes bore a 5-cent cover price. They appeared under a 1010 series number and had an all-picture comic strip interior. Similar to these were the 845, 1058, and 1066 series devoted to Walt Disney characters.

Several other variant forms of BLBs, including Penny Books,® Feature Movie Books® and many of the children's paint books and storybooks, often considered BLBs, are included in this guide.

Fast Action® and *Dime Action*® Books

In 1936, Whitman published a set of four titles for Dell Publishing Company. These books appeared in both a varnished, hardcover 15-cent edition (6833) and an unvarnished, soft-cover 10-cent edition (unnumbered). The first type was called Cartoon Story Books,® while the second, Fast Action Stories.® Both editions had 240 pages and measured 4 x 5¼ x 7/10 inches. In 1938, the series was revived, but the Cartoon Story Book® edition was dropped. From 1938-1943, thirty-three additional Fast-Action Story® BLBs were produced. In 1941, numbering began with 8 and continued until the series ended in 1943, with 16. Curiously, 15 (*The Adventures of Andy Panda*) has a later copyright date (1943) than 16 (*Mickey Mouse and Pluto*), which is dated 1942. Because of their esoteric nature, Fast-Action® BLBs bring very good prices.

In 1941, Fawcett Publishing Company produced four titles identical in format to the Fast-Action Stories.® These Dime Action® books also sold for ten cents, and are valuable mainly because of the characters they featured (Bulletman, Captain Marvel, Minute Man, and Spy Smasher).

The Big Little Book® Market

There are many places where Big Little Books® can be found. If you are fortunate, you may find them at thrift shops and used book dealers for a fraction of their value. At local auctions in rural settings boxes of these books used to sell for fifty cents a box. No one wanted these books, then. Now, most of these cheap sources have been tapped dry, particularly in the last ten years.

There are two more common sources for BLBs today. The first is the comic book dealer, who often carries Big Little Books® as well as related items. A dealer saves you the time of looking for the books you need, but in return generally asks for a premium price. For those collectors who cannot afford this service, or for those who are more adventuresome, try local antique dealers. Often these dealers have purchased BLBs inexpensively and can pass them along at an affordable price. To the collector, this type of seek-and-find is particularly rewarding. But beware—many dealers suspect a Big Little Book® is more valuable than it really is and will overprice the book.

Determinants of Value

Value for whatever one collects depends on desirability. There are several determinants of desirability for a particular BLB.

Main Character. While the condition of a BLB is the ultimate determining factor of desirability, probably the first thing one looks for in Big Little Books® is the main character. The collector recognizes certain characters as prominent and popular, and realizes that BLBs with these characters command higher prices. The more desirable characters, usually represented in the comic strips of that time, include Buck Rogers, Dick Tracy, Donald Duck, Flash Gordon, Little Orphan Annie, Mickey Mouse, Popeye, and Tarzan. There are, however, several characters, like Roy Rogers, Red Ryder, and Gene Autry, that were highly popular, but bring only moderate prices. This situation may be temporary, as many of these titles, particularly westerns, are experiencing rekindled popularity. On the other hand, there are titles that were not that popular, but bring very high prices now. Notable among these are Charlie Chan and Green Hornet BLBs. The Shadow and Tom Mix books are perfect examples of noncomic strip characters of high popularity and equally high prices.

Artists. In many cases, the popularity of the main character is dependent on the ability of the artist who drew him. Certainly the best example of this is the high popularity of Flash Gordon and Jungle Jim, and their artist Alex Raymond. In other cases, the character has developed popularity almost in spite of the artist's style—as the early Buck Rogers and Dick Tracy titles would prove. In these instances, the artist, while not the most talented, presented an exciting concept in a novel way. The art tends to grow on you. Sometimes the artist makes the book desirable despite content. A good example of this is the recent popularity of books illustrated by Henry Vallely.

In any case, one can assume that in collecting BLBs the better the artwork, the greater the value. Aside from Raymond and Vallely, some of the better artists include Allen Dean, who drew the King of the Royal Mounted books; Al Capp, who drew Li'l Abner; Alfred Andriola of Kerry Drake fame, who also did the Charlie Chan BLBs; Milton Caniff of Terry and the Pirates; and Will Gould of Red Barry, whose fantastic mixture of Raymond-and-Caniff-style drawings are underrated. There are, of course, many other good artists, like Harold Gray, Walt Disney, Fred Harman, Elzie Segar, Bud Sagandorf, Roy Crane, and Jim Gary, among others. In short, the greatness of the artist largely depends on personal tastes, and that is the ultimate factor in building a collection. This guide attempts to include all artists for this reason, and all artwork that can be identified is so noted.

Scarcity. The degree of difficulty in locating certain Big Little Books® has much to do with their value. Naturally, the harder a book is to find, the more it is sought after, and the more it will bring on the market.

The scarcity of any BLB rests on factors like pressrun and age. Fast-Action® and Dime Action® books, miniatures, giveaways, and other variants had both lower print runs and distribution. Generally, those that were not distributed were destroyed. Many of the books made prior to, and during, World War II were destroyed through paper drives. Oversized and unusual-sized BLBs, such as Big Big Books,® Feature Movie Books,® and Paramount Newsreel,® are hard to find because they were overlooked at the store—either because of their high price or because they weren't recognized as Big Little Books.®

The following terms are used in this guide to define scarcity. Because research in the BLB field is relatively new, precise numbers are difficult to determine. Consequently, the breakdown is comparatively wide. As more information becomes available, certain books may change status.

Scarce: 500-1000 copies
Very scarce: 100-500 copies
Rare: 50-100 copies
Very rare: fewer than 50 copies

Esoterica. Much the same way fans develop for science fiction, fantasy, mystery, horror, and spy genres, so it is with Big Little Books.® Many collectors specialize in some area of interest in the BLB field. There are many forms of esoteric Big Little Books.® These include books dealing with crime, science fiction, war, and movies; books with unusual titles or characters, like *The Ghost Avenger,* or the Charlie Chan books; books containing "flip movies"; Walt Disney or Walter Lantz books; miniatures and giveaways; oversized books; and books containing works by certain artists. All of these things, and more, have their own place among collectors. As a result, regional interests for certain esoteric forms of BLBs can cause prices to fluctuate, depending on demand.

Condition and Grading. An obviously important determinant of value is the condition of Big Little Books.® Many of the earlier BLBs are plagued with defects — missing pages, fading covers, pencil markings, crayon or paint, missing cover or spine. Often BLBs are found with a combination of these defects. The desirability and value of such books quickly diminishes. Pieces missing in the spine and cover and missing pages of text are the most damaging. In comparison, if these pages are missing, the flaw is minor: blank inside pages, title pages, or the additional Big Little Books® pages (found at the back of a book). Yet, a combination of minor defects can subtract substantially from a book's value.

The following grading system categorizes the various defects commonly found in BLBs and relates them, in a practical manner, to the book's condition. It must be noted that because of the fragile nature of Big Little Books,® that is, the tendency for corners to bend and chip at the slightest mishandling, most BLBs had some defect even when new. For this reason, copies are seldom found in pristine mint condition. It should be noted as well that overgrading occurs frequently in buying and selling BLBs. Therefore, it must be emphasized that one must adhere strictly to the grading information when pricing books.

Pristine Mint (PM)	A totally flawless copy. Perfect in every way. No fading on the cover, no color chipping along the edges. Spine, cover, and pages are perfectly flat. Book is stiff when opened and pages are white. BLBs in this condition are hardly ever found and bring prices of up to 100 percent over mint for desirable titles. Warehouse copies.
Mint (M)	BLBs found in mint condition are almost perfect. Mint copies bear no obvious flaws. However, they need not be stiff when opened. Very slight color flaking (one or two) allowable, but no other defects.
Near Mint (NM)	Minor color chipping along spine or edges. Still no obvious signs of wear. A carefully read copy, still flat, with no creases in cover or spine. Cover still lustrous.

Very Fine (VF)   Color chipping more noticeable, with slight discoloration of pages allowable. Book corners may curve inward. No pages missing. Cover colors are not as sharp as in mint condition. Original owner's name and address may be penciled in on the inside of the book.

Fine (F)   Slight tearing at the joints of the spine or corners of the cover. Pages may be yellowing slightly. Cover and spine still tight. Minor tearing of a page or two allowable. May be missing only one of the blank inside pages. Wear visible, but not heavy. Owner's name may be inked in, but only if done in an attractive manner.

Very Good (VG)   May be missing both inside blank pages, or one of the pages with the list of other BLBs, or a coupon page—but not all of these. Yellowing of the pages or browning along the edges of the pages okay. Cover fading and minor pieces of the spine missing. Still a complete book with, perhaps, cover and spine loose, but connected.

Good (G)   Up to half the spine missing, or a portion of the cover missing allowable, only if not combined with several other defects. May have minor coloring of the pages with crayon or other material. Title page and blank pages may be missing. May have the last illustration of the story missing, but no missing text. Lightly browning, but nonbrittle pages. Cover fading and wear may be noticeable. Spine may be unhinged on one side. Corners rolled inward. A couple of pages may be torn.

Fair (Fa)   Heavy wear and fading. Browned pages. Coloring with crayons or paint may occur frequently. Has both front and back cover, at least, but may be missing spine. These are filler books, with perhaps a few pages missing, including text pages. Generally, all books with missing spines fall into this category. If the book has no other flaws, its value is approximately 80 percent of a book in good condition. Otherwise, most fair copies are worth no more than 60 percent of a book in good condition.

Poor (P)   A ragged book. Even a book with covers and pages intact may be graded as poor if there are other serious defects. A copy missing an entire cover is considered poor. This is a book with brown, brittle pages, coloring, and pages missing. It is useless to dealers and to most collectors and is never worth more than 20 percent of a book in good condition unless (1) it is a hard-to-obtain book; or (2) it is a mint book, missing the cover only. In such cases, it may be worth up to 50 percent of a book in good condition.

How to Store Your Big Little Books®

Big Little Books® should be cared for like any other paper collectible. For best possible care, BLBs should be wrapped individually with an inert plastic, like Mylar, and should be shelved upright, side by side, with enough room between each book to keep them from rubbing together. When removing from the shelf, take care not to pull the book by the spine. If books are to be stored, BLBs should be placed in acid-free cardboard boxes, still upright. All paper should be kept cool and dry for best preservation.

Terminology

The following terms are used for reference in this guide.

all-pix (all picture). Books that contain only pictures and no text.

BLB (Big Little Book®). Used generically to cover all books in this guide, though technically only the Whitman books were called such.

FA (Fast-Action®). Books having a BLB format, but printed by Whitman for Dell Publishing Company.

FM (flip movie). BLBs that contain small pictures in an upper corner of every page. The pages were flipped with the thumb to give the impression of motion. Generally, flip movie BLBs are harder to find in better condition as most had bent covers from use.

hc (hardcover). Board-covered books. Most BLBs had hard, or stiff, covers. However, Saalfield books were available in both hard and softbound versions.

min (miniature). Softbound BLBs that were smaller in format than the regular issues.

movie. Books containing photos from movies.

nn (no number). Books produced without a series number.

oversized. Books that were larger in format than the regular issues. Designated by (O).

pre (premium). Giveaway BLBs.

sc (soft cover). BLBs with soft bindings.

sty (story). Refers to story content.

Whitman Publishing Company

Whitman Publishing Company
Racine, Wisconsin

Because of the wide variety of Big Little Books® published by Whitman, titles are grouped alphabetically, in sections, in the following manner: Big Little® and Better Little Books® (1932-1949); New Better Little Books® (1949-1950); The Big Little Book TV Series® (1958); A Big Little Book® (1967-1969, 1973-present); Variant Big Little Books® (1933-1943, including Big Big Books,® Big Little Nickel Books,® Famous Comics,® Famous Comics Cartoon Books,® Famous Funnies Cartoon Books,® Dell's Fast Action Stories® and Cartoon Story Books,® Nickel Books,® Penny Books,® Tall Comic Books,® Top-Line Comics,® Wee Little Books,® miniatures, giveaways, and miscellaneous books).

Big Little® *and Better Little Books*® *(1932-1949)*

Big Little Books® contained four sets of numbered series titles: a 700 series, two 1100 series, one 1400 series, and one book, *Clyde Beatty with Lions and Tigers,* numbered 653. Better Little Books® contained five additional 1400 series. Many books from the two 1100 series and the six 1400 series bear identical numbers.

The following entries, like all of those in this book, are arranged whenever possible as follows: series number; title of book; author; artist; nature and characteristics of book (whether movie, all-picture, flip movie feature, and so on); and publication date. This information is followed by three grades—good, fine, mint—with the corresponding market value for each. Books with (O) after the series number have oversized formats. When a book is written and illustrated by the same person, or when the artist is unknown, only the author's name follows the title, unless otherwise stated.

1177 *Ace Drummond.* Capt. Eddie Rickenbacker, Clayton Knight art, 1935.
$10 $15 $22

1448 *Air Fighters of America.* Roy J. Snell, Robert Jenney art, FM, 1941.
$8 $12 $18

759 (O) *Alice in Wonderland.* From Louis Carroll, Paramount movie, hc with sc spine, 1934.
$10 $20 $30

1481 *Allen Pike of the Parachute Squad, U.S.A.* Russell R. Winterbotham, Erwin L. Hess art, FM, 1941.
$7 $12 $17

763 *Alley Oop and Dinny.* V.T. Hamlin, first Alley Oop BLB, 1935.
$10 $15 $30

1473 *Alley Oop and Dinny in the Jungles of Moo.* V.T. Hamlin, 1938.
$9 $14 $27

1431 *Andy Panda and the Mad Dog Mystery.* Walter Lantz Productions, 1947.
$8 $12 $20

1459 *Andy Panda and the Pirate Ghosts.* Walter Lantz Productions, 1949.
$8 $12 $20

1425 *Andy Panda and Tiny Tom.* Walter Lantz Productions, all-pix, first Andy Panda BLB, 1944.
$9 $14 $27

1441 *Andy Panda in the City of Ice.* Walter Lantz Productions, all-pix, 1948.
$8 $12 $20

1485 *Andy Panda's Vacation.* Walter Lantz Productions, all-pix, 1946.
$8 $12 $20

1130 *Apple Mary and Dennie Foil the Swindlers.* Martha Orr, reprints from first Mary Worth strips, 1936.
$10 $15 $25

1403 *Apple Mary and Dennie's Lucky Apples.* Martha Orr, 1939.
$8 $12 $20

1192 *Arizona Kid on the Bandit Trail.* Peter Maple, Hal Arbo cover and art, 1936.
$8 $12 $20

1469 *Bambi.* Adapted from Felix Salten, Walt Disney Studios, 1942.
$10 $25 $40

1497 *Bambi's Children.* From Felix Salten, Walt Disney Studios, FM, 1943.
$9 $20 $30

1459 *Barney Baxter in the Air with the Eagle Squadron.* Frank Miller, 1938.
$8 $12 $20

760 (O) *Believe It or Not.* Robert Ripley, hc with sc spine, 1933.
$10 $20 $30

1158 (O) *Betty Boop in Miss Gulliver's Travels.* Max Fleischer cartoon, Wallace West sty, hc with sc spine, 1935.
$10 $22 $35

1119 (O) *Betty Boop in Snow White.* Max Fleischer cartoon, Wallace West sty, hc with sc spine, 1934.
$12 $25 $40

1119 (O) *Betty Boop in Snow White.* As above, only soft-cover version, 1934.
$15 $30 $45

1443 *Big Chief Wahoo (and the Great Gusto).* Allen Saunders and Elmer Woggon, 1938.
$6 $12 $18

1432 *Big Chief Wahoo and the Lost Pioneers.* Allen Saunders and Elmer Woggon, FM, 1942.
$5 $10 $15

1483 *Big Chief Wahoo and the Magic Lamp.* Allen Saunders and Elmer Woggon, first FM book, 1942.
$5 $10 $15

725 (O) *Big Little Mother Goose.* Very scarce, sc, 576 pages, 1934.
$10 $22 $40

725 (O) *Big Little Mother Goose.* As above, except cover illustration variation, 1934.
$10 $22 $40

725 (O) *Big Little Mother Goose.* As above, except hc and cover illustration variation. Some found with hc over sc, 1934.
$12 $25 $45

721 (O) *Big Little Paint Book.* Rare, 336 pages, sc, 1934.
$15 $30 $55

721 (O) *Big Little Paint Book.* As above, except hc and 320 pages, 1934.
$15 $30 $55

773 *Billy the Kid.* Leon Morgan, 1934.
$5 $10 $15

1414 *Black Silver and His Pirate Crew (with Tom Trojan).* Extreme violence, 1937.
$8 $16 $24

1447 *Blaze Brandon with the Foreign Legion.* Gaylord R. DuBois, Robert Weisman cover and art, 1938.
$5 $10 $15

1415 *Blondie and Baby Dumpling.* Chic Young, 1937.
$7 $14 $21

1429 *Blondie and Baby Dumpling.* Chic Young, character's name misspelled as "Bumpstead." Cover title is probably a mistake. Inside says "Blondie with Baby Dumpling and Daisy," 1939.
$9 $17 $26

1476 *Blondie and Bouncing Baby Dumpling.* Chic Young, 1940.
$7 $14 $21

1438 *Blondie and Dagwood, Everybody's Happy.* Chic Young, 1948.
$7 $14 $21

1410 *Blondie and Dagwood in Hot Water.* Chic Young, 1946.
$7 $14 $21

1487 *Blondie, Baby Dumpling and All.* Chic Young, FM, 1941.
$7 $14 $21

1491 *Blondie, Cookie and Daisy's Pups.* Chic Young, 432 pages, 1943.
$7 $14 $21

1491 *Blondie, Cookie and Daisy's Pups.* As above, except 352 pages with ads on back cover and inside, 1943.
$9 $18 $27

1430 *Blondie, Count Cookie in Too!* Chic Young, 1947.
$7 $14 $21

1463 *Blondie, Fun for All.* Chic Young, 1949.
$6 $12 $18

1450 Blondie, No Dull Moments. Chic Young, 1948.
$6 $12 $18

1466 Blondie, or Life Among the Bumsteads. Chic Young, 1944.
$7 $14 $21

1490 Blondie, Papa Knows Best. Chic Young, 1945.
$7 $14 $21

1423 Blondie, Who's Boss? Chic Young, 1942.
$7 $14 $21

1419 Blondie, The Bumsteads Carry On. Chic Young, 1941.
$7 $14 $21

1432 Bob Stone, The Young Detective. Peter K. Maple, Henry E. Vallely cover, crime photos, 1937.
$6 $12 $18

1108 Bobby Benson on the H-Bar-O Ranch. Peter Dixon, 1934.
$8 $16 $24

1425 Brad Turner in Transatlantic Flight. Albert B. Dale, Robert Jenney art, 1939.
$7 $14 $21

1427 Brenda Starr and the Masked Imposter. Dale Messick, 1940.
$8 $16 $24

1426 Brer Rabbit. Walt Disney Studios, from Joel Chandler Harris, all-pix, 1947.
$7 $14 $21

1480 Brick Barton and the Winning Eleven, Coach Bernie Bierman's. Coach Bernie Bierman, R.M. Williamson art, 1938.
$5 $10 $15

1480 Brick Barton and the Winning Eleven, Coach Bernie Bierman's. As above, except a transition book, BLB logo blacked out, 1938.
$7 $14 $21

1468 Brick Bradford with Brocco the Modern Buccaneer. William Ritt and Clarence Gray, 1938.
$6 $12 $18

1133 *Bringing Up Father.* George McManus, 1936.
$10 $20 $30

1417 *Bronc Peeler, The Lone Cowboy.* Fred Harman, 1937.
$7 $13 $20

1470 *Buccaneer, The.* Paramount movie with Fredric March, Walter Brennan and Anthony Quinn, Cecil B. DeMille picture, 1938.
$9 $18 $27

1451 *Buck Jones and the Killers of Crooked Butte.* Gaylord DuBois, 1940.
$6 $12 $18

1461 *Buck Jones and the Rock Creek Cattle War.* Gaylord DuBois, Al Lewin and Ken Ernst art, 1938.
$6 $12 $18

1461 *Buck Jones and the Rock Creek Cattle War.* As above, except transition book, BLB logo blacked out, 1938.
$8 $16 $24

1486 *Buck Jones and the Rough Riders in Forbidden Trails, with Tim McCoy and Raymond Hatton.* Monogram movie-based, FM, 1943.
$7 $14 $21

1404 *Buck Jones and the Two-Gun Kid.* Gaylord DuBois, Robert Weisman art, 1937.
$8 $15 $23

1116 *Buck Jones in Ride'Em Cowboy.* Universal movie, written originally by Buck Jones, 1937.
$8 $16 $24

1104 (O) *Buck Jones in The Fighting Code.* Pat Patterson, Columbia movie, first Buck Jones BLB, 1934.
$9 $18 $27

1188 *Buck Jones in The Fighting Rangers.* Universal movie, 1936.
$8 $16 $24

1169 *Buck Rogers and the Depth Men of Jupiter.* Dick Calkins and Phil Nowlan, 1935.
$20 $30 $55

1175 *Buck Rogers and the Doom Comet.* Dick Calkins and Phil Nowlan, 1936.
$15 $22 $35

1474 *Buck Rogers and the Overturned World.* Dick Calkins and Phil Nowlan, FM, 1941.
$15 $22 $35

1197 *Buck Rogers and the Planetoid Plot.* Dick Calkins and Phil Nowlan, Nowlan's name misspelled as "Nolan," 1936.
$18 $25 $45

1490 *Buck Rogers and the Super-Dwarf of Space.* Dick Calkins and Phil Nowlan, all-pix, 1943.
$15 $22 $35

765 *Buck Rogers in the City Below the Sea.* Dick Calkins and Phil Nowlan, scarce, 1934.
$25 $40 $75

1437 *Buck Rogers in the War with the Planet Venus.* Dick Calkins and Phil Nowlan, 1938.
$18 $25 $45

1143 *Buck Rogers on the Moons of Saturn.* Dick Calkins and Phil Nowlan, cover scuffs easily, 1934.
$20 $35 $60

nn *Buck Rogers on the Moons of Saturn.* As above, except sc with different three-color cover illustration, 1934.
$25 $40 $70

742 *Buck Rogers, 25th Century A.D.* Dick Calkins and Phil Nowlan, first Buck Rogers BLB, 1933.
$20 $30 $55

1409 *Buck Rogers, 25th Century A.D. VS the Fiend of Space.* Dick Calkins and Phil Nowlan, 1940.
$15 $22 $35

713 *Buffalo Bill and the Pony Express.* Leon Morgan, Hal Arbo art, 1934.
$5 $10 $15

1194 *Buffalo Bill Plays a Lone Hand.* Buck Wilson, Hal Arbo art, 1936.
$5 $10 $15

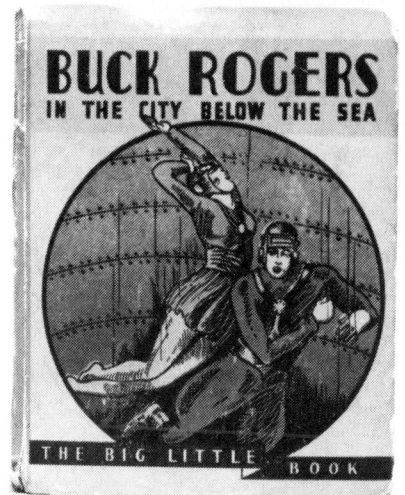

1435 *Bugs Bunny.* Leon Schlesinger Productions, all-pix, first Bugs Bunny BLB, 1943.
$8 $15 $23

1496 *Bugs Bunny and His Pals.* Warner Brothers Cartoon, all-pix, 1945.
$6 $12 $18

1455 *Bugs Bunny and Klondike Gold.* Warner Brothers Cartoon, 1948.
$6 $12 $18

1403 *Bugs Bunny and the Pirate Loot.* Warner Brothers Cartoon, all-pix, 1947.
$6 $12 $18

1440 *Bugs Bunny in Risky Business.* Warner Brothers Cartoon, all-pix, 1948.
$6 $12 $18

1465 *Bugs Bunny, The Masked Marvel.* Warner Brothers Cartoon, 1949.
$6 $12 $18

1415 *Buz Sawyer and Bomber 13.* Roy Crane, 1946.
$8 $15 $23

1412 *Calling W-1-X-Y-Z Jimmy Kean and the Radio Spies.* Thorp McClusky, Sam Nisenson art, 1939.
$6 $12 $18

1474 *Captain Easy, Behind Enemy Lines.* Roy Crane, 1943.
$8 $16 $24

1128 *Captain Easy, Soldier of Fortune.* Roy Crane, 1934.
$9 $18 $27

nn *Captain Easy, Soldier of Fortune.* As above, except sc with different three-color cover illustration, 1934.
$11 $22 $35

1444 *Captain Frank Hawks, Air Ace and the League of Twelve.* Irwin Meyers art, 1938.
$7 $13 $20

1402 *Captain Midnight and Sheik Jomak Khan.* Helen Berke, 1946.
$10 $20 $30

1452 *Captain Midnight and the Moon Woman.* 1943.
$10 $20 $30

1488 *Captain Midnight and the Secret Squadron VS the Terror of the Orient.* Russell R. Winterbotham, Erwin L. Hess art, FM, first Captain Midnight BLB, 1942.
       $15 $23 $35

1478 *Charlie Chan, Inspector of the Honolulu Police.* Earl Derr Biggers, Alfred Andriola art, 1939.
       $20 $30 $45

1459 *Charlie Chan Solves a New Mystery.* Earl Derr Biggers, Alfred Andriola art, 1940.
       $15 $23 $35

1424 *Charlie Chan, Villiany on the High Seas, Inspector.* Earl Derr Biggers, Alfred Andriola art, FM, 1942.
       $10 $20 $30

1456 *Charlie McCarthy and Edgar Bergen, Story of.* Eleanor Packer, Henry Vallely art, 1938.
       $10 $20 $30

734 *Chester Gump at Silver Creek Ranch.* Sidney Smith, first BLB to use an encircled logo on cover, 1933.
       $8 $15 $23

nn *Chester Gump at Silver Creek Ranch.* As above, except sc, 1933.
       $10 $20 $30

766 *Chester Gump Finds the Hidden Treasure.* Sidney Smith, 1934.
       $7 $14 $21

1146 *Chester Gump in the City of Gold.* Sidney Smith, 1935.
       $7 $14 $21

nn *Chester Gump in the City of Gold.* As above, except sc with different three-color cover illustration, 1935.
       $9 $18 $27

1402 *Chester Gump in the Pole to Pole Flight.* Sidney Smith, 1937.
       $6 $12 $18

1453 *Chuck Malloy Railroad Detective on the Streamliner.* Thorp McClusky, Joseph R. Kress art, 1938.
       $6 $12 $18

1410 *Clyde Beatty, Daredevil Lion and Tiger Tamer.* Gaylord DuBois, 1938.
$7　$14　$21

653 (O) *Clyde Beatty, Lions and Tigers with the Sensational Dare-Devil.* From the Universal movie *The Big Cage*, 1934.
$10　$20　$35

1446 *Convoy Patrol (A Thrilling U.S. Navy Story).* Russell R. Winterbotham, Erwin L. Hess art, FM, 1942.
$5　$10　$15

1457 *Cowboy Lingo.* Fred Harman, 1938.
$6　$12　$18

724 *Cowboy Stories.* Leon Morgan, Hal Arbo art, 1933.
$6　$12　$18

1125 *Dan Dunn on the Trail of the Counterfeiters.* Norman Marsh, 1936.
$8　$15　$23

1116 *Dan Dunn Secret Operative 48.* Norman Marsh, first Dan Dunn BLB, 1934.
$9　$17　$25

1481 *Dan Dunn Secret Operative 48 and the Border Smugglers.* Norman Marsh, 1938.
$7　$14　$21

1171 *Dan Dunn Secret Operative 48 and the Crime Master.* Norman Marsh, 1937.
$7　$14　$21

1492 *Dan Dunn Secret Operative 48 and the Dope Ring.* Norman Marsh, 1940.
$12　$24　$35

1417 *Dan Dunn Secret Operative 48 and the Underworld Gorillas.* Norman Marsh, all-pix with two FMs, 1937.
$7　$14　$21

1454 *Dan Dunn Secret Operative 48 on the Trail of Wu Fang.* Norman Marsh, 1938.
$7　$14　$21

Row one: *Apple Mary and Dennie Foil the Swindlers,* **F**, $15; *Billy the Kid's Pledge (Saalfield),* **M**, $11; *Blondie and Baby Dumpling (1939),* **VF**, $20; *Blondie, Count Cookie in Too!,* **M**, $21; *Brer Rabbit,* **NM**, $19; *Broncho Bill (Saalfield),* **NM**, $12.
Row two: *The Buccaneer,* **M**, $27; *Buck Rogers and the Planetoid Plot,* **VG+**, $21; *Buck Rogers in the City Below the Sea,* **VG**, $32; *Buck Jones and the Killers of Crooked Butte,* **F+**, $14.
Row three: *Buffalo Bill Plays a Lone Hand,* **M**, $15; *Buz Sawyer and Bomber 13,* **NM**, $21; *Broncho Bill (Whitman Tarzan Ice-Cream Cup-Lid premium),* **NM** $28; *Buck Rogers and the Depth Men of Jupiter,* **VG**, $25.
Row four: *Bud Shinners and the Oregon Trail (Samuel Lowe),* **M**, $8; *Bugs Bunny, Accidental Adventure (A Big Little Book),* **M**, $5.

NOTE: All books in the Color Section are Whitman, unless otherwise noted.

Row one: *Captain Frank Hawks, Air Ace, and the League of Twelve,* **VG+, $10;** *Chuck Malloy, Railroad Detective on the Streamliner,* **VF, $15;** *Cowboy Malloy (Saalfield),* **M, $11;** *Dan Dunn, Secret Operative 48, and the Crime Master,* **F+, $16;** *Danger Trails in Africa,* **M, $18;** *The Desert Eagle and the Hidden Fortress,* **VF+, $15.**
Row two: *Dick Tracy and the Spider Gang,* **VG, $17;** *Dick Tracy and Yogee Yamma,* **VF+, $22;** *Doctor Doom Faces Death at Dawn (International Spy),* **F, $14;** *Don O'Dare Finds War,* **F, $11.**
Row three: *Don Winslow and the Giant Girl Spy,* **NM, $20;** *Erik Noble and the Forty-Niners,* **M, $27;** *The Story of Dippy the Goof (Walt Disney Hardbound, 1066 series),* **VF, $13;** *Dick Whittington and His Cat (1104 series Penny Book),* **VF, $6.**
Row four: *Cinderella and the Magic Wand (New Better Little Book),* **VG, $9;** *Danny Meets the Cowboys (Samuel Lowe),* **M, $8.**

NOTE: All books in the Color Section are Whitman, unless otherwise noted.

Row one: *Flash Gordon and the Monsters of Mongo*, **VG**, **$25**; *Flash Gordon and the Tournaments of Mongo*, **VG+**, **$27**; *Flash Gordon and the Witch Queen of Mongo*, **VG**, **$25**; *Flash Gordon in the Water World of Mongo*, **VG**, **$24**; *Freckles and the Lost Diamond Mine*, **VG+**, **$12**; *G-Man, Breaking the Gambling Ring*, **VG+**, **$12**.
Row two: *G-Men on the Job*, **NM**, **$15**; *Gene Autry and the Mystery of Paint Rock Canyon*, **M**, **$16**; *Ghost Avenger*, **VF**, **$17**; *The Adventures of Huckleberry Finn*, **M**, **$16**.
Row three: *Inspector Wade Solves the Mystery of the Red Aces*, **NM**, **$14**; *Houdini's Big Little Book® of Magic (Cocomalt premium)*, **VG**, **$14**; *Flipper, Deep Sea Photographer (A Big Little Book®)*, **M**, **$5**; *The Gingerbread Boy (1104 series Penny Book)*, **VF**, **$6**.
Row four: *Fun, Puzzles, Riddles (1100B series Penny Book)*, **F**, **$4**; *Goofy in Giant Trouble (A Big Little Book®)*, **M**, **$5**; *Flint Adams and the Stage Coach (Samuel Lowe)*, **M**, **$8**.

NOTE: All books in the Color Section are Whitman, unless otherwise noted.

Row one: *Jack Swift and His Rocket Ship,* **G+**, **$9**; *Jim Craig, State Trooper, and the Kidnapped Governor,* **VF+**, **$11**; *Jim Starr of the Border Patrol,* **VF**, **$11**; *Jimmie Allen in the Air Mail Robbery,* **F**, **$10**; *Jungle Jim,* **F**, **$18**; *Kayo and Moon Mullins and the One Man Gang,* **VF**, **$13**.
Row two: *Keep 'Em Flying U.S.A. for America's Defense,* **NM**, **$10**; *Junior Nebb on the Diamond Bar Ranch (transition book),* **F+**, **$16**; *King of the Royal Mounted and the Northern Treasure,* **F+**, **$14**; *King of the Royal Mounted Gets His Man,* **F+**, **$14**.
Row three: *Little Orphan Annie and the Big Train Robbery,* **VF**, **$20**; *Little Orphan Annie and the Gooneyville Mystery,* **M**, **$20**; *Little Orphan Annie and the Secret of the Well,* **M**, **$20**; *Little Minister (Engel-Van Wiseman),* **G+**, **$14**.
Row four: *Little Tex in the Midst of Trouble (Samuel Lowe),* **M**, **$8**; *Great Expectations (Engel-Van Wiseman),* **NM**, **$28**.

NOTE: All books in the Color Section are Whitman, unless otherwise noted.

Row one: *The Lone Ranger and His Horse Silver,* **VG, $15;** *The Lone Ranger and the Red Renegades,* **VG+, $11;** *Lone Star Martin of the Texas Rangers,* **NM, $10;** *Mac of the Marines in Africa,* **VG, $9;** *Mandrake the Magician and the Flame Pearls,* **VG+, $10;** *Men with Wings,* **F, $8.**
Row two: *Mickey Mouse and Bobo the Elephant,* **VG+, $15;** *Mickey Mouse and the Bat Bandit,* **VG, $23;** *Mickey Mouse Runs His Own Newspaper,* **VF+, $20;** *Speed Douglas and the Mole Gang,* **VF, $13.**
Row three: *Moon Mullins and Kayo,* **F, $13;** *Our Gang Adventures,* **M, $22;** *$1000 Reward, (Saalfield),* **NM, $16;** *Lassie and the Shabby Sheik (A Big Little Book®),* **M, $5.**
Row four: *Micky Mouse, Adventure in Outer Space (A Big Little Book®),* **M, $7;** *The Mail Must Go Through (Samuel Lowe),* **M, $8.**

NOTE: All books in the Color Section are Whitman, unless otherwise noted.

Row one: *Pat Nelson, Ace of the Test Pilots*, **VF, $10;** *Perry Winkle and the Rinkeydinks Get a Horse*, **VG+, $10;** *Pluto the Pup*, **NM, $23;** *Popeye and Castor Oyl the Detective*, **NM, $23;** *Popeye and the Deep Sea Mystery*, **M, $30;** *Popeye and the Jeep*, **M, $30.**
Row two: *Popeye in Quest of His Poopdeck Pappy*, **M, $30;** *Pioneers of the Wild West (World Syndicate, blue cover)*, **NM, $19;** *Pioneers of the Wild West (World Syndicate, red cover)*, **NM, $23;** *Paramount Newsreel Men with Admiral Byrd in Little America*, **VG, $13.**
Row three: *Pinocchio and Jiminy Cricket (Dell Fast Action®)*, **G+, $23;** *Mickey's Dog Pluto (Tall Comic)*, **G, $12;** *Nevada Jones, Trouble Shooter (Samuel Lowe)*, **M, $8;** *Popeye's Ark (Saalfield)*, **FA, $6.**
Row four: *The Outlaw's Last Ride (Samuel Lowe)*, **M, $8;** *Popeye, Ghost Ship to Treasure Island (A Big Little Book®)*, **VF, $6.**

NOTE: All books in the Color Section are Whitman, unless otherwise noted.

Row one: *Red Barry, Undercover Man,* **VG+**, **$8**; *The Red Death on the Range,* **VF**, **$13**; *Red Ryder and Circus Luck,* **M**, **$13**; *Red Ryder and Little Beaver,* **VG**, **$15**; *Red Ryder and the Rimrock Killer,* **NM**, **$12**; *Red Ryder and the Squaw-Tooth Rustlers,* **M**, **$15**.
Row two: *Reg'lar Fellers,* **F**, **$11**; *Reg'lar Fellers (Cocomalt premium),* **F**, **$18**; *Roy Rogers in Robbers' Roost,* **M**, **$15**; *Secret Agent X-9,* **F+**, **$23**.
Row three: *Sequoia,* **VG+**, **$13**; *Shooting Sheriffs (of the Wild West),* **VF**, **$9**; *Red Ryder, Acting Sheriff (New Better Little Book),* **VF+**, **$13**; *Smokey Stover, The False Alarm Fireman,* **F**, **$13**.
Row four: *Smitty, Golden Gloves Tournament (Cocomalt premium),* **F**, **$20**; *Smokey Stover, The Foo Fighter,* **VG+**, **$16**; *Smilin' Jack and the Jungle Pipe Line,* **NM**, **$14**.

NOTE: All books in the Color Section are Whitman, unless otherwise noted.

Row one: *Sombrero Pete,* **F, $9;** *Spook Riders on the Overland (Saalfield),* **VG+, $9;** *Tarzan, Lord of the Jungle,* **F, $14;** *The Tarzan Twins,* **VG+, $19;** *Tex Thorne Comes Out of the West,* **F, $13;** *Terry and the Pirates, Shipwrecked on a Desert Island,* **F, $13.**
Row two: *Terry Lee, Flight Officer U.S.A.,* **M, $20;** *Tim McCoy and the Sandy Gulch Stampede,* **F, $11;** *Tim Tyler's Luck and the Plot of the Exiled King,* **VG, $10;** *Tom Beatty, Ace of the Service, Scores Again,* **F, $11;** *Sir Lancelot (The Big Little Book® TV Series),* **NM, $14.**
Row three: *Wash Tubbs and Captain Easy, Hunting for Whales,* **F, $11;** *Tailspin Tommy (Tarzan Ice-Cream Cup-Lid premium),* **VG+, $20;** *Tom Mix in the Fighting Cowboy,* **VG+, $13;** *The Son of the Phantom (Whitman Mystery and Adventure Hardback Series),* **VF+, $12.**
Row four: *Tailspin Tommy, The Pay-Roll Mystery (rectangular premium, with ad on back cover),* **Fa+, $10;** *The Three Musketeers (Feature Movie Book — listed in regular Whitman titles),* **VG, $18;** *The Steel Arena (Saalfield),* **VF+, $14.**
Row five: *Tarzan (Tarzan Ice-Cream Cup-Lid premium),* **G, $15.**

NOTE: All books in the Color Section are Whitman, unless otherwise noted.

1151 *Danger Trails in Africa.* Martin Johnson, 1935.
$6 $12 $18

1148 (O) *David Copperfield.* Eleanor Packer, MGM movie with W.C. Fields, hc with sc spine, 1934.
$8 $15 $23

1148 (O) *David Copperfield.* As above, except sc, 1934.
$8 $15 $23

1431 *Desert Eagle and the Hidden Fortress.* James O. Parsons, J.R. White art, FM, 1941.
$6 $11 $17

1458 *Desert Eagle Rides Again.* John W. Finney, J.R. Nisenson art, FM, 1939.
$7 $13 $20

1484 *Detective Higgins of the Racket Squad.* Millard Thackson, Herbert Anderson art, 1938.
$7 $14 $21

707 *Dick Tracy, Adventures of.* Chester Gould, first BLB, 1932.
$15 $30 $45

710 *Dick Tracy and Dick Tracy Junior.* Chester Gould, 1933.
$12 $24 $36

1439 *Dick Tracy and His G-Men.* Chester Gould, FM, 1941.
$10 $20 $30

1445 *Dick Tracy and the Bicycle Gang.* Helen Berke, Chester Gould art, 1948.
$8 $16 $24

1163 *Dick Tracy and the Boris Arson Gang.* Chester Gould, 1935.
$10 $20 $30

1163 *Dick Tracy and the Boris Arson Gang.* As above, but with an upside-down cover, 1935.
$11 $22 $33

1420 *Dick Tracy and the Hotel Murders.* Chester Gould, 1937.
$10 $20 $30

1435 *Dick Tracy and the Mad Killer.* Helen Berke, Chester Gould art, 1947.
$8 $16 $24

41

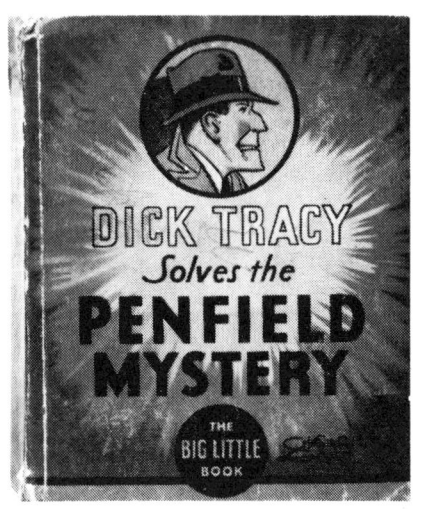

1491   *Dick Tracy and the Man with No Face*. Chester Gould, 1938.
$10 $20 $30

1491   *Dick Tracy and the Man with No Face*. As above, except transition book, BLB logo blacked out, 1938.
$13 $25 $37

1434   *Dick Tracy and the Phantom Ship*. Chester Gould, 1940.
$9 $18 $27

1112   *Dick Tracy and the Racketeer Gang*. Chester Gould, 1936.
$10 $20 $30

1446   *Dick Tracy and the Spider Gang, Detective*. Republic Pictures movie serial with Ralph Byrd, 1937.
$11 $22 $33

1105   *Dick Tracy and the Stolen Bonds*. Chester Gould, 1934.
$10 $20 $30

1460   *Dick Tracy and the Tiger Lily Gang*. Helen Berke, Chester Gould art, 1949.
$8 $16 $24

1482   *Dick Tracy and the Wreath Kidnaping Case*. Chester Gould, 1946.
$9 $18 $27

1412   *Dick Tracy and Yogee Yamma*. Helen Berke, Chester Gould art, 1946.
$8 $16 $24

749   *Dick Tracy, From Colorado to Nova Scotia*. Chester Gould, 1933.
$10 $20 $30

749   *Dick Tracy, From Colorado to Nova Scotia*. As above, except sc, 1933.
$11 $22 $33

1185   *Dick Tracy in Chains of Crime*. Chester Gould, 1936.
$10 $20 $30

1454   *Dick Tracy on the High Seas*. Chester Gould, 1938.
$10 $20 $30

1170   *Dick Tracy on the Trail of Larceny Lu*. Chester Gould, 1935.
$10 $20 $30

1478 *Dick Tracy on Voodoo Island.* Chester Gould, 1944.
$9 $18 $27

723 *Dick Tracy Out West.* Chester Gould, 1933.
$12 $24 $36

1495 *Dick Tracy Returns.* Chester Gould, movie based, 1939.
$10 $20 $30

1137 *Dick Tracy Solves the Penfield Mystery.* Chester Gould, 1934.
$10 $20 $30

nn *Dick Tracy Solves the Penfield Mystery.* As above, except sc with a different three-color cover illustration, 1934.
$15 $27 $40

1449 *Dick Tracy Special F.B.I. Operative.* Chester Gould, 1943.
$9 $18 $27

1488 *Dick Tracy, The Super-Detective.* Chester Gould, 1939.
$10 $20 $30

1479 *Dick Tracy VS Crooks in Disguise.* Chester Gould, FM, 1939.
$10 $20 $30

1124 *Dickie Moore in the Little Red Schoolhouse.* Chesterfield Pictures, 1936.
$8 $16 $24

1464 *Dirigible ZR-90 and the Disappearing Zeppelin, Captain Roff of.* Russell R. Winterbotham, Al Lewin art, 1941.
$7 $14 $21

1460 *Doctor Doom and the Ghost Submarine, Foreign Spies.* Conrad Vane, Al McWilliams art, 1939.
$7 $14 $21

1148 *Doctor Doom Faces Death at Dawn, International Spy.* Conrad Vane, Hal Arbo cover, 1937.
$7 $14 $21

1438 *Don O'Dare Finds War.* Gaylord DuBois, Erwin L. Hess art, 1940.
$6 $11 $17

1408 *Don Winslow and the Giant Girl Spy.* Frank V. Martinek, 1946.
$7 $14 $21

1418 *Don Winslow Navy Intelligence Ace.* Frank V. Martinek, FM, 1942.
$8 $16 $24

1489 *Don Winslow of the Navy and the Great War Plot.* Frank V. Martinek, 1940.
$9 $18 $27

1453 *Don Winslow of the Navy and the Secret Enemy Base.* Frank V. Martinek, 1943.
$8 $16 $24

1419 *Don Winslow of the Navy VS the Scorpion Gang.* Frank V. Martinek, 1938.
$9 $18 $27

1107 *Don Winslow, U.S.N., Lieutenant Commander.* Frank V. Martinek, first Don Winslow BLB, I.A. Beroth art, 1935.
$11 $22 $33

nn *Don Winslow, U.S.N., Lieutenant Commander.* As above, except sc with a different three-color cover illustration, 1935.
$14 $28 $42

1411 *Donald Duck and Ghost Morgan's Treasure.* Carl Barks sty and art, reprint of comic book *Four-Color 9,* all-pix, 1946.
$20 $35 $45

1432 *Donald Duck and the Green Serpent.* Carl Barks sty and art, all-pix, 1947.
$15 $30 $40

1462 *Donald Duck Gets Fed Up.* Al Taliaferro, 1938.
$9 $18 $27

1430 *Donald Duck Headed for Trouble.* Al Taliaferro, FM, 1942.
$7 $14 $21

1478 *Donald Duck Hunting for Trouble.* Al Taliaferro, 1938.
$7 $14 $21

1478 *Donald Duck Hunting for Trouble.* As above, except a transition book, BLB logo blacked out, 1938.
$10 $20 $30

1457 *Donald Duck in Volcano Valley.* Carl Barks sty and art, 1949.
$7 $14 $21

1484 *Donald Duck Is Here Again.* Al Taliaferro, all-pix, 1944.
$8 $16 $24

1449 *Donald Duck Lays Down the Law.* Carl Barks sty and art, 1948.
$7 $14 $21

1438 *Donald Duck Off the Beam.* Al Taliaferro, 424 pages, left-handed FM, 1943.
$8 $16 $24

1438 *Donald Duck Off the Beam.* As above, except shorter version (352 pages) and ads on back cover and inside, 1943.
$8 $16 $24

1424 *Donald Duck Says Such Luck!* Al Taliaferro, FM, 1941.
$7 $14 $21

1422 *Donald Duck Sees Stars.* Al Taliaferro, FM, 1941.
$7 $14 $21

1404 *Donald Duck Says Such a Life!* Al Taliaferro, 1939.
$7 $14 $21

1486 *Donald Duck Up in the Air.* Carl Barks sty and art, 1945.
$7 $14 $21

1434 *Donald Forgets to Duck.* Al Taliaferro, cover used for the Fast Action *Donald Out of Luck,* 1939.
$8 $16 $24

1416 *Draftie of the U.S. Army.* Paul Foggerty, all-pix, 1943.
$6 $12 $18

1400 *Dumbo, The Flying Elephant.* Walt Disney Studios, based on cartoon, FM, 1942.
$8 $16 $24

774 (O) *Eddie Cantor, An Hour with You.* Movie, based on several Ziegfield-Goldwyn movies, 1934.
$10 $20 $30

1106 *Ella Cinders and the Mysterious House.* Bill Conselman and Charlie Plumb, 1934.
$8 $15 $23

1406 *Ellery Queen in the Adventure of the Last Man Club.* Ellery Queen, 1940.
$12 $24 $36

1472 *Ellery Queen, The Adventure of the Murdered Millionaire.* Ellery Queen, adapted from Fred Dannay and Manfred Lee, Erwin L. Hess art, FM, 1942.
$10 $20 $30

772 *Erik Noble and the Forty-Niners.* Lloyd E. Smith, B. McNaughton art, 1934.
$9 $18 $27

nn *Erik Noble and the Forty-Niners.* As above, except sc with a different three-color cover illustration, 1934.
$12 $24 $36

1129 *Felix the Cat.* Adapted from Pat Sullivan, 1936.
$15 $25 $40

1439 *Felix the Cat.* All-pix, 1943.
$10 $20 $30

1465 *Felix the Cat.* All-pix, 1945.
$8 $16 $24

1401 *Fighting Heroes Battle for Freedom.* Stookie Allen, all-pix, 1943.
$5 $10 $15

1464 *Flame Boy and the Indians' Secret.* Oren Arnold, art by Sekakuku, a Hopi Indian artist, 1938.
$5 $10 $15

1447 *Flash Gordon and the Fiery Desert of Mongo.* Alex Raymond, 1948.
$15 $20 $25

1166 *Flash Gordon and the Monsters of Mongo.* Alex Raymond, 1935.
$20 $30 $40

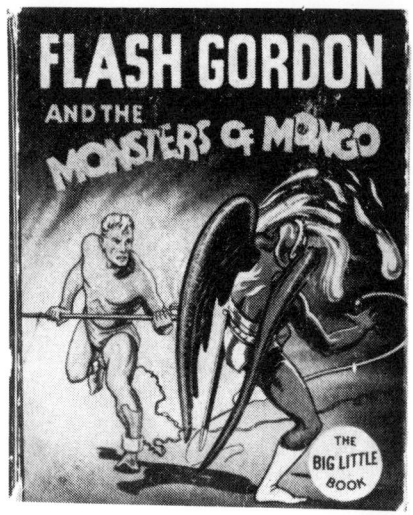

nn *Flash Gordon and the Monsters of Mongo.* As above, except sc with a different three-color cover illustration, 1935.
$22 $35 $45

1423 *Flash Gordon and the Perils of Mongo.* Alex Raymond, 1940.
$18 $25 $30

1469 *Flash Gordon and the Power Men of Mongo.* Alex Raymond, 1943.
$15 $20 $25

1479 *Flash Gordon and the Red Sword Invaders.* Alex Raymond, 1945.
$15 $20 $25

1171 *Flash Gordon and the Tournaments of Mongo.* Alex Raymond, 1935.
$20 $30 $40

1484 *Flash Gordon and the Tyrant of Mongo.* Alex Raymond, FM, 1942.
$15 $20 $25

1190 *Flash Gordon and the Witch Queen of Mongo.* Alex Raymond, 1936.
$20 $27 $35

1492 *Flash Gordon in the Forest Kingdom of Mongo.* Alex Raymond, 1938.
$20 $27 $35

1443 *Flash Gordon in the Ice World of Mongo.* Alex Raymond, left-handed FM, 1942.
$15 $20 $25

1424 *Flash Gordon in the Jungles of Mongo.* Alex Raymond, 1947.
$12 $18 $24

1407 *Flash Gordon in the Water World of Mongo.* Alex Raymond, 1937.
$20 $27 $35

1110 *Flash Gordon on the Planet Mongo.* Alex Raymond, first Flash Gordon BLB, 1934.
$25 $45 $60

1467 *Flint Roper and the Six-Gun Showdown.* Glenn F. Chesnut, 1941.
$5 $10 $15

1175 *Frank Buck Presents Ted Towers, Animal Master.* Glen Cravath, 1935.
$7 $11 $15

1121 *Frank Merriwell at Yale.* Burt L. Standish, Jack R. Wilhelm art, 1935.
$5 $9 $11

1164 *Freckles and the Lost Diamond Mine.* Merrill Blosser, 1937.
$7 $14 $21

1469 *G-Man and the Gun Runners.* George Clark and Lou Hanlon, 1940.
$7 $11 $15

1434 *G-Man and the Radio Bank Robberies.* Allen Dale, Herbert Anderson art, 1937.
$8 $14 $20

1493 *G-Man Breaking the Gambling Ring.* Russell R. Winterbotham, Jim Gary art, 1938.
$8 $14 $20

1118 *G-Man on the Crime Trail.* George Clark and Lou Hanlon, 1936.
$8 $12 $16

1147 *G-Man VS the Red X.* 1936.
$8 $14 $20

1470 *G-Man VS the Fifth Column.* Edwin C. Johnson, J.R. White art, FM, 1941.
$7 $11 $15

1168 *G-Men on the Job.* Dick Blair, Milt Youngren art, 1935.
$8 $12 $16

1451 *Gang Busters in Action.* Isaac McAnally, Henry Vallely art, 1938.
$10 $16 $22

1451 *Gang Busters in Action.* As above, except a transition book, BLB logo blacked out, 1938.
$12 $20 $26

1437 *Gang Busters Smash Through.* Gene Fletcher, Russ Stamm art, 1942.
$7 $11 $15

1433 *Gang Busters Step In.* Isaac McAnally, Henry Vallely art, from Phillips H. Lord's radio program, 1939.
$8 $14 $20

1409 *Gene Autry and Raiders of the Range.* Till Goodan, 1946.
$8 $12 $16

1493 *Gene Autry and the Hawk of the Hills.* H.C. Thomas, Vallely art, left-handed FM, 1942.
$8 $12 $16

1434 *Gene Autry and the Gun-Smoke Reckoning.* Wilton West, Irwin Meyers art, 1943.
$8 $12 $16

1439 *Gene Autry and the Land Grab Mystery.* 1945.
$8 $12 $16

1425 *Gene Autry and the Mystery of Paint Rock Canyon.* Bob Beaugrand, 1947.
$8 $12 $16

1461 *Gene Autry and the Red Bandit's Ghost.* 1949.
$7 $11 $15

1494 *Gene Autry Cowboy Detective.* Russell R. Winterbotham, Erwin L. Hess art, 1940.
$8 $14 $20

1483 *Gene Autry in Law of the Range.* Gaylord DuBois, Al Lewin art, 1939.
$8 $14 $20

1433 *Gene Autry in Public Cowboy No. 1.* Eleanor Packer, Republic movie, first Gene Autry BLB, 1938.
$10 $20 $30

1456 *Gene Autry in Special Ranger Rule.* H.C. Thomas, Henry Vallely art, 1941.
$8 $12 $16

1428 *Gene Autry—Special Ranger.* H.C. Thomas, Erwin L. Hess art, FM, 1941.
$8 $12 $16

1457 *George O'Brien and the Hooded Riders.* Gaylord DuBois, Erwin L. Hess art, 1940.
$7 $11 $15

1418 *George O'Brien in Gun Law.* Eleanor Packer, RKO movie, 1935.
$8 $14 $20

1462 *Ghost Avenger (Strikes).* Russell R. Winterbotham, Henry Vallely art, FM, 1943.
$10 $15 $20

1480 *Green Hornet Cracks Down.* Fran Striker, Henry Vallely art, FM, 1942.
$10 $15 $20

1496 *Green Hornet Returns.* Fran Striker, FM, 1941.
$10 $15 $20

1453 *Green Hornet Strikes!* Fran Striker, Robert Weisman art, 1940.
$14 $19 $25

776 (O) *Gun Justice.* Starring Ken Maynard, Universal movie, hc with sc spine, 1934.
$9 $16 $23

776 (O) *Gun Justice.* As above, except sc version, 1934.
$10 $18 $27

1426 *Guns in the Roaring West.* Steve Saxton, 1937.
$5 $8 $12

1101 *Hairbreadth Harry in Department Q.T.* Alexander, last 384-page BLB, soft-type cover, 1935.
$7 $10 $15

1101 *Hairbreadth Harry in Department Q.T.* As above, except harder cover, 1935.
$7 $10 $15

1413 *Hal Hardy in the Lost Land of Giants (The World 1,000,000 Years Ago).* R.B. Winter, 1938.
$7 $10 $15

1159 *Hall of Fame of the Air.* Eddie Rickenbacker, Clayton Knight art, 1936.
$5 $8 $11

1145 (O) *Hap Lee's Selection of Movie Gags.* Illustrations of about 100 photos of movie stars, plus caricatures, hc with sc spine, 1935.
$10 $16 $25

1418 *Harold Teen Swinging at the Sugar Bowl.* Carl Ed, 1939.
$6 $9 $15

715 *Houdini's Big Little Book of Magic.* From a 1927 book by Harry Houdini, 1933.
$10 $15 $20

1422 *Huckleberry Finn, The Adventures of.* From Mark Twain, excellent Henry Vallely art, 1939.
$8 $12 $16

1155 *In the Name of the Law.* William Engle, 1937.
$6 $11 $14

1448 *Inspector Wade Solves the Mystery of the Red Aces.* Lyman Anderson, Hal Arbo cover, adapted from Edgar Wallace, 1937.
$7 $10 $15

1403 *Invisible Scarlet O'Neil.* Russell Stamm, all-pix, two FMs, 1942.
$9 $13 $19

1406 *Invisible Scarlet O'Neil Versus the King of the Slums.* Russell Stamm, 1946.
$7 $10 $15

1435 *Jack Armstrong and the Ivory Treasure.* Leslie N. Daniels, Jr., Henry Vallely art, 1937.
$7 $10 $15

1432 *Jack Armstrong and the Mystery of the Iron Key.* Based on radio program, Henry Vallely art, 1939.
$7 $9 $14

1102 *Jack Swift and His Rocket Ship.* Cliff Farrell and Hal Colson, 1934.
$7 $11 $16

1402 *Jackie Cooper in Gangster's Boy.* Karl Brown and Robert D. Andrews, Monogram movie, 1938.
$8 $14 $20

714 *Jackie Cooper, Movie Star of Skippy and Sooky.* Eleanor Packer, movie photos, 1933.
$9 $16 $23

1490 *Jane Arden, The Vanished Princess.* Monte Barrett art, Russell Ross sty, 1938.
      $6 $10 $15

1463 *Jane Withers in Keep Smiling.* Eleanor Packer, Twentieth Century-Fox movie, 1938.
      $7 $11 $16

1179 *Jane Withers in This Is the Life.* Eleanor Packer, Twentieth Century-Fox movie, 1937.
      $8 $12 $17

1424 *Jaragu of the Jungle.* Rex Beach, excellent William Mark Young art, 1937.
      $9 $14 $20

1447 *Jerry Parker Police Reporter and the Candid Camera Clue.* Jack Wallen, Emilie Wallen art, 1941.
      $6 $8 $11

1466 *Jim Craig State Trooper and the Kidnapped Governor.* Steve Saxton, Herbert Anderson art, 1938.
      $6 $9 $13

1428 *Jim Starr of the Border Patrol.* Oren Arnold, Herbert Anderson art, 1937.
      $6 $9 $12

1143 *Jimmie Allen in the Air Mail Robbery.* Willfred G. Moore and Robert M. Burtt, 1936.
      $7 $10 $14

1105 *Joe Louis, The Brown Bomber.* Gene Kessler, World Wide Press photos, unusual, 1936.
      $9 $14 $20

1123 *Joe Palooka, The Heavyweight Boxing Champ.* Ham Fisher, 1934.
      $8 $13 $19

1402 *John Carter of Mars.* Edgar Rice Burroughs, John Coleman Burroughs cover and art, 1940.
      $20 $30 $40

1493 *Judy Garland and Mickey Rooney.* Movie scenes, 1941.
      $7 $13 $22

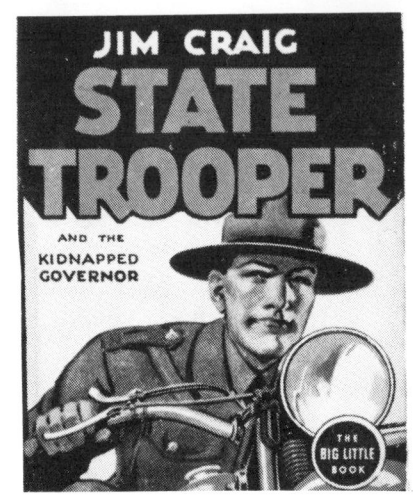
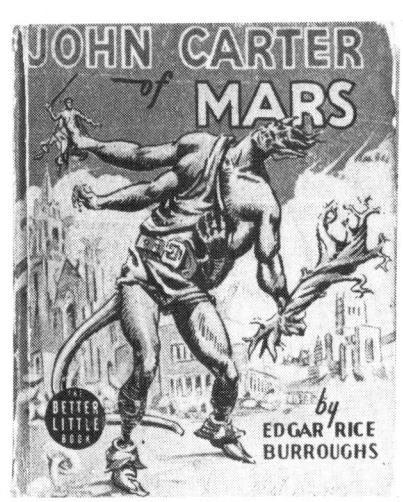

1138 *Jungle Jim.* Alex Raymond, 1936.
$13 $18 $25

1139 *Jungle Jim and the Vampire Woman.* Alex Raymond, 1937.
$10 $15 $20

1442 *Junior G-Men.* Morrell Massey, superb Henry Vallely art, 1937.
$8 $10 $14

1470 *Junior Nebb Joins the Circus.* Sol Hess, 1939.
$8 $10 $14

1422 *Junior Nebb on the Diamond Bar Ranch.* Sol Hess, 1938.
$8 $16 $24

1422 *Junior Nebb on the Diamond Bar Ranch.* As above, except a transition book, BLB logo blacked out, more common, 1938.
$7 $14 $20

1401 *Just Kids.* Ad Carter, 1937.
$8 $11 $15

1411 *Kay Darcy and the Mystery Hideout.* Irene Ray, Charles Mueller art, 1937.
$5 $9 $13

1415 *Kayo and Moon Mullins and the One Man Gang.* Frank Willard, 1939.
$7 $11 $16

1180 *Kayo in the Land of Sunshine.* Frank Willard, 1937.
$6 $9 $11

1105 *Kazan in Revenge of the North.* James Oliver Curwood, Henry Vallely art, 1937.
$7 $11 $14

1471 *Kazan, King of the Pack.* James Oliver Curwood, Erwin L. Hess art, 1940.
$7 $9 $12

1420 *Keep 'Em Flying U.S.A. for America's Defense.* Russell R. Winterbotham, Henry Vallely art, FM, 1943.
$5 $8 $11

1442 *Ken Maynard and the Gun Wolves of the Gila.* Gaylord DuBois, Gene Baxter art, 1939.
$8 $13 $18

1430 *Ken Maynard in Western Justice.* Rex Loomis, Irwin Meyers art, 1938.
$8 $11 $16

1103 *King of the Royal Mounted.* Zane Grey, 1936.
$9 $15 $23

1486 *King of the Royal Mounted and the Great Jewel Mystery.* Zane Grey, 1939.
$7 $11 $16

1179 *King of the Royal Mounted and the Northern Treasure.* Beautiful Allen Dean art, from Zane Grey, 1937.
$8 $13 $19

1452 *King of the Royal Mounted Gets His Man.* Zane Grey, beautiful Allen Dean art, 1938.
$8 $13 $19

1405 *King of the Royal Mounted—The Long Arm of the Law.* Zane Grey, all-pix, two FMs, 1943.
$7 $10 $14

1132 (O) *Last Days of Pompeii.* A Feature Movie Book® produced under the BLB 1100 series, RKO movie starring Preston Foster, sc, 1935.
$13 $20 $30

1125 *Laughing Dragon of Oz.* Frank Baum, Milt Youngren art, scarce, 1934.
$15 $24 $35

1441 *Lightning Jim U.S. Marshall Brings Law to the West.* Albert Macale, radio based, 1940.
$5 $8 $12

1401 *Li'l Abner Among the Millionaires.* Al Capp, 1939.
$9 $14 $20

1198 *Li'l Abner in New York.* Al Capp, 1936.
$12 $18 $26

1117 *Little Annie Rooney and the Orphan House.* Brandon Walsh, 1936.
$5 $8 $12

1406 *Little Annie Rooney on the Highway to Adventure.* Brandon Walsh, 1938.
$5 $8 $12

1429 *Little Lulu, Alvin and Tubby, Marge's.* Marjorie H. Buell, all-pix, 1947.
$9 $14 $20

1150 (O) *Little Men.* Eleanor Packer, Mascot movie starring F. Darro and Ralph Morgan, adapted from Louisa May Alcott, with both hard and soft spines, 1934.
$9 $14 $20

1120 *Little Miss Muffet.* Fanny Y. Cory, 1936.
$7 $11 $16

708 *Little Orphan Annie.* Harold Gray, first Little Orphan Annie BLB, 1928 strip copyright date, but published in 1933.
$25 $40 $53

748 *Little Orphan Annie and Chizzler.* Harold Gray, 1933.
$16 $26 $35

1457 *Little Orphan Annie and Her Junior Commandos.* Harold Gray, 1943.
$8 $13 $19

1162 *Little Orphan Annie and Punjab the Wizard.* Harold Gray, 1935.
$16 $26 $35

716 *Little Orphan Annie and Sandy.* Harold Gray, 1933.
$20 $31 $43

1414 *Little Orphan Annie and the Ancient Treasure of Am.* Harold Gray, 432 pages, 1939.
$14 $23 $30

1468 *Little Orphan Annie and the Ancient Treasure of Am.* Harold Gray, 288 pages, dated 1939, but a reissue of above, last Better Little Book,® 1949.
$8 $13 $19

1140 *Little Orphan Annie and the Big Train Robbery.* Harold Gray, 1934.
$12 $18 $25

nn *Little Orphan Annie and the Big Train Robbery.* As above, except sc with a different three-color cover illustration, 1934.
$24 $33 $45

1154 *Little Orphan Annie and the Ghost Gang.* Harold Gray, 1935.
$12 $18 $25

nn *Little Orphan Annie and the Ghost Gang.* As above, except sc with a different three-color cover illustration, 1935.
$20 $29 $40

1435 *Little Orphan Annie and the Gooneyville Mystery.* Helen Berke, Harold Gray art, 1947.
$10 $14 $20

1482 *Little Orphan Annie and the Haunted Mansion.* Harold Gray, FM, 1941.
$12 $18 $25

1449 *Little Orphan Annie and the Mysterious Shoemaker.* Harold Gray, 1938.
$10 $14 $20

1186 *Little Orphan Annie and the $1,000,000 Formula.* Harold Gray, 1936.
$12 $18 $25

1417 *Little Orphan Annie and the Secret of the Well.* Helen Berke, Harold Gray art, 1947.
$10 $14 $20

1461 *Little Orphan Annie and the Underground Hide-out.* Harold Gray, 1945.
$10 $14 $20

1416 *Little Orphan Annie in the Movies.* Harold Gray, 1937.
$14 $23 $30

1446 *Little Orphan Annie in the Thieves' Den.* Berke, Harold Gray art, 1948.
$10 $14 $20

1103 *Little Orphan Annie with the Circus.* Harold Gray, 1934.
$14 $23 $30

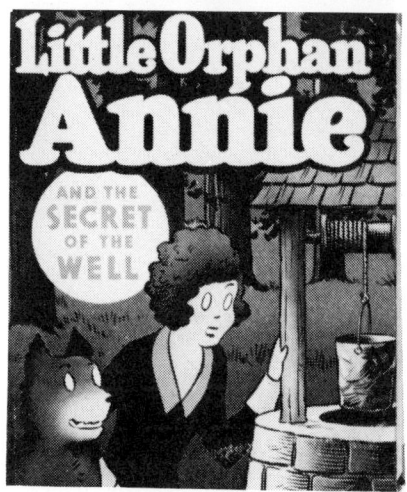

757 (O) *Little Women.* RKO movie with Katherine Hepburn, adapted from Louisa May Alcott, hc with sc spine, 1934.
$10 $14 $20

1407 *Lone Ranger and Dead Men's Mine.* Fran Striker, 1939.
$8 $13 $19

1181 *Lone Ranger and His Horse Silver.* Based on radio program, Hal Arbo art, first Lone Ranger BLB, 1935.
$12 $18 $25

1450 *Lone Ranger and the Black Shirt Highwayman.* Fran Striker, 1939.
$8 $13 $19

1477 *Lone Ranger and the Great Western Span.* Fran Striker, Henry Vallely art, FM, 1942.
$10 $14 $20

1465 *Lone Ranger and the Menace of Murder Valley.* Buck Wilson, Robert R. Weisman art, 1937.
$7 $11 $16

1489 *Lone Ranger and the Red Renegades.* Fran Striker, 1939.
$8 $13 $19

1431 *Lone Ranger and the Secret Killer.* Buck Wilson, Herbert Anderson art, 1937.
$7 $11 $16

1428 *Lone Ranger and the Secret Weapon.* Fran Striker, Henry Vallely art, 1943.
$7 $11 $16

1498 *Lone Ranger and the Silver Bullets.* Fran Striker, Henry Vallely art, Hal Arbo cover, 1946.
$7 $11 $16

1196 *Lone Ranger and the Vanishing Herd.* Buck Wilson, William Juhre art, 1936.
$10 $14 $20

1468 *Lone Ranger Follows Through.* Fran Striker, Henry Vallely art, 1941.
$8 $13 $19

1421 *Lone Ranger on the Barbary Coast.* Fran Striker, Henry Vallely art, 1944.
$7 $11 $16

1405 *Lone Star Martin of the Texas Rangers.* Peter A. Wyckoff, Ted Horn art, 1939.
$5 $9 $11

753 (O) *Lost Patrol, The.* RKO movie with Boris Karloff and Victor McLagen, 1934.
$12 $18 $25

1189 *Mac of the Marines in Africa.* Mark Smith, 1936.
$7 $11 $16

1400 *Mac of the Marines in China.* Mark Smith, Frank J. Hoban art, 1938.
$7 $11 $16

1167 *Mandrake the Magician.* Lee Falk and Phil Davis, 1935.
$12 $18 $25

1418 *Mandrake the Magician and the Flame Pearls.* Lee Falk and Phil Davis, 1946.
$7 $11 $16

1431 *Mandrake the Magician and the Midnight Monster.* Lee Falk and Phil Davis, 1939.
$8 $13 $19

1454 *Mandrake the Magician, Mighty Solver of Mysteries.* Lee Falk and Phil Davis, FM, 1941.
$7 $11 $16

1438 *Mary Lee and the Mystery of the Indian Beads.* Alice Anderson, 1937.
$5 $8 $12

1436 *Maximo, The Amazing Superman.* Russell R. Winterbotham, Henry Vallely art, 1941.
$7 $11 $16

1444 *Maximo, The Amazing Superman and the Crystals of Doom.* Russell R. Winterbotham, Henry Vallely art, FM, 1941
$7 $11 $16

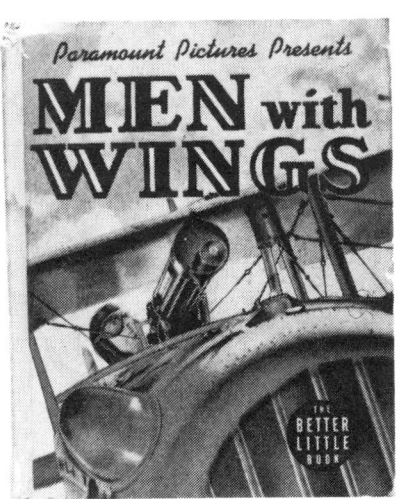
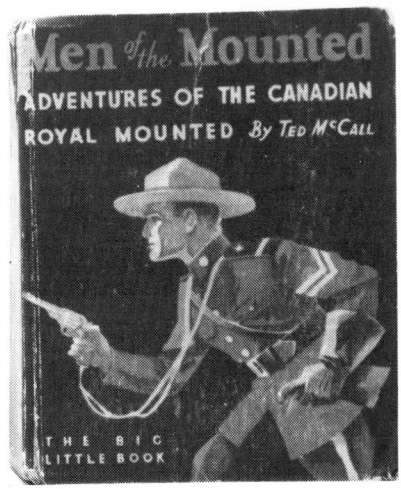

1445 *Maximo, The Amazing Superman and the Super-Machine.* Russell R. Winterbotham, Henry Vallely art, FM, 1941.
$7 $11 $16

755 *Men of the Mounted.* Ted McCall, 1934.
$7 $11 $16

1475 *Men with Wings.* Eleanor Packer, Paramount movie with Fred MacMurray and Ray Milland, 1938.
$5 $8 $12

717 *Mickey Mouse.* Floyd Gottfredson sty and art, first Mickey Mouse BLB, Mickey looks like a rat, Walt Disney cover (?), scarce, 1933.
$35 $60 $80

717 *Mickey Mouse.* As above, except a different cover, more like the modern Mickey Mouse image, very scarce, 1933.
$45 $80 $100

1160 *Mickey Mouse and Bobo the Elephant.* Floyd Gottfredson, 1935.
$12 $18 $26

1128 *Mickey Mouse and Pluto the Racer.* Floyd Gottfredson, 1936.
$10 $17 $25

1153 *Mickey Mouse and the Bat Bandit.* Floyd Gottfredson, slight racial pun—Chinese cook called "Chinky," 1935.
$17 $27 $36

nn *Mickey Mouse and the Bat Bandit.* As above, except sc with a different three-color cover illustration, 1935.
$30 $45 $65

1451 *Mickey Mouse and the Desert Palace.* Floyd Gottfredson, 1948.
$10 $14 $20

1471 *Mickey Mouse and the Dude Ranch Bandits.* Floyd Gottfredson, 432 pages, Merrill de Maris sty, FM, 1943.
$17 $27 $36

1471 *Mickey Mouse and the Dude Ranch Bandits.* As above, except 352 pages, ads on back cover and inside, 1943.
$12 $18 $25

1433 *Mickey Mouse and the Lazy Daisy Mystery.* Floyd Gottfredson, 1947.
$10 $14 $20

1413 *Mickey Mouse and the 'Lectro Box.* Floyd Gottfredson, 1946.
$10 $14 $20

1429 *Mickey Mouse and the Magic Lamp.* Floyd Gottfredson, FM, 1942.
$14 $23 $30

1463 *Mickey Mouse and the Pirate Submarine.* Floyd Gottfredson, 1939.
$17 $27 $36

1187 *Mickey Mouse and the Sacred Jewel.* Floyd Gottfredson, 1936.
$14 $23 $30

1475 *Mickey Mouse and the Seven Ghosts.* Floyd Gottfredson, 1940.
$17 $27 $36

1464 *Mickey Mouse in the Stolen Jewels.* Floyd Gottfredson, 1949.
$10 $14 $20

1483 *Mickey Mouse, Bell Boy Detective.* Floyd Gottfredson, 1945.
$12 $18 $25

726 *Mickey Mouse in Blaggard Castle.* Floyd Gottfredson, 1934.
$14 $23 $30

1428 *Mickey Mouse in the Foreign Legion.* Floyd Gottfredson, 1940.
$14 $23 $30

1476 *Mickey Mouse in the Race for Riches.* Floyd Gottfredson, FM, a transition book with the words "Big Little Book" still on logo, very scarce, 1938.
$20 $30 $40

1476 *Mickey Mouse in the Race for Riches.* As above, except a transition book with BLB logo blacked out, 1938.
$12 $18 $25

1476 *Mickey Mouse in the Race for Riches.* As above, except a transition book with the Better Little Book logo imprint, 1938.
$12 $18 $25

1401 *Mickey Mouse in the Treasure Hunt.* Floyd Gottfredson, left-handed FM, 1941.
$14 $23 $30

1444 *Mickey Mouse in World of Tomorrow.* Floyd Gottfredson, 1948.
$12 $18 $25

1417 *Mickey Mouse on Sky Island.* Floyd Gottfredson, new style Mickey, minus the triangular pie wedges in the eyes, FM, 1941.
$17 $27 $36

1499 *Mickey Mouse on the Cave-Man Island.* Merrill de Maris sty, Floyd Gottfredson art, 1944.
$12 $18 $26

756 (O) *Mickey Mouse Presents a Walt Disney Silly Symphony.* Walt Disney Studios, scarce, 1933.
$25 $37 $50

1409 *Mickey Mouse Runs His Own Newspaper.* Floyd Gottfredson, 1937.
$12 $18 $25

750 *Mickey Mouse Sails for Treasure Island.* Floyd Gottfredson, scarce, 1933.
$20 $30 $40

1139 *Mickey Mouse, The Detective.* Floyd Gottfredson, first appearance of Dippy (later Goofy), 1934.
$17 $27 $36

nn *Mickey Mouse, The Detective.* As above, except sc edition, 1934.
$25 $40 $60

731 *Mickey Mouse, The Mail Pilot.* Floyd Gottfredson, hc with sc spine, 320 pages, 1933.
$12 $18 $25

731 *Mickey Mouse, The Mail Pilot.* As above, except a different size, 3½ x 4⅞ x 1¼ inches, 1933.
$17 $27 $36

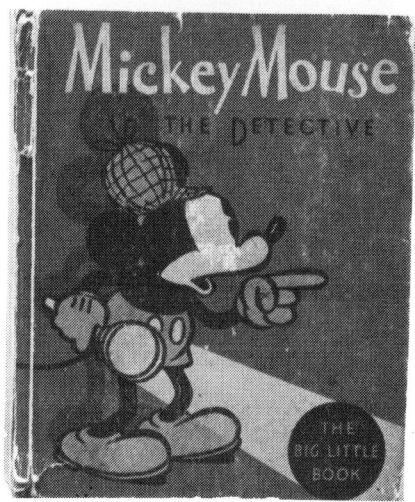

731 *Mickey Mouse, The Mail Pilot.* As above, except 4 x 4⅜ x 1½ inches and 300 pages, 1933.
$17 $27 $36

731 *Mickey Mouse, The Mail Pilot.* As above, except sc and 4 x 4⅞ x ⅞ inches, 1933.
$14 $23 $30

1493 *Mickey Rooney and Judy Garland (and How They Got into the Movies).* Edward I. Gruskin, Henry Vallely art, 1941.
$14 $23 $30

1427 *Mickey Rooney, Himself.* Eleanor Packer, MGM movie, last Whitman movie BLB, 1939.
$10 $14 $20

710 (O) *Moby Dick (or the Great White Whale).* Warner Brothers movie with John Barrymore, hc with sc spine, 1934.
$10 $14 $20

746 *Moon Mullins and Kayo.* Frank Willard, hc with sc spine, unusual experimental red-tone title page, inside says "Kayo and Moon Mullins," first Moon Mullins BLB, 1933.
$9 $13 $19

1134 *Moon Mullins and the Plushbottom Twins.* Frank Willard, 1935.
$10 $14 $20

nn *Moon Mullins and the Plushbottom Twins.* As above, except sc with a different three-color cover illustration, 1935.
$17 $27 $36

1408 *Mr. District Attorney on the Job.* Based on Phillips H. Lord's radio program, contains two stories, FM, 1941.
$7 $11 $15

1113 *Mutt and Jeff.* Bud Fisher, 1934.
$20 $30 $40

1497 *Myra North Special Nurse and Foreign Spies.* Charles Coll, Ray Thompson art, 1938.
$7 $11 $15

1400 *Nancy and Sluggo.* Ernie Bushmiller, all-pix, 1946.
$14 $23 $30

1487 *Nancy Has Fun.* Ernie Bushmiller, all-pix, 1944.
$12 $18 $25

1115 *Og, Son of Fire.* Irving Crump, based on radio program, 1936.
$5 $9 $12

718 *Once Upon a Time.* W.J. Enright, sc, rounded corners, page edges stained green, 1933.
$10 $15 $22

1403 *Oswald Rabbit Plays G-Man.* Walter Lantz, adapted by Eleanor Packer from a Universal cartoon, 1937.
$7 $11 $15

1109 (O) *Oswald, The Lucky Rabbit.* Carl Laemmle, from a Universal cartoon, hc with sc spine, 1934.
$15 $25 $33

1456 *Our Gang Adventures.* Based on MGM serials, Walt Kelly art (?), 1948.
$10 $15 $22

1451 *Our Gang on the March.* Eleanor Packer, Henry Vallely art, left-handed FM, three story lines from MGM movie, 1942.
$7 $11 $15

1118 (O) *Paramount Newsreel Men with Admiral Byrd in Little America.* Oversized, with photos, designed as a teaching aid, not as a BLB, but format has since classified it as a BLB, 1934.
$10 $14 $20

1445 *Pat Nelson, Ace of Test Pilots.* Dougal Lee, 1937.
$5 $9 $11

1463 *Peggy Brown and the Jewel of Fire.* Kathryn Heisenfelt, Henry Vallely art, 1943.
$7 $11 $15

1411 *Peggy Brown and the Mystery Basket.* Kathryn Heisenfelt, Henry Vallely art, FM, 1941.
$8 $12 $17

1427 *Peggy Brown and the Runaway Auto Trailer.* Kathryn Heisenfelt, Henry Vallely art, 1937.
$8 $13 $18

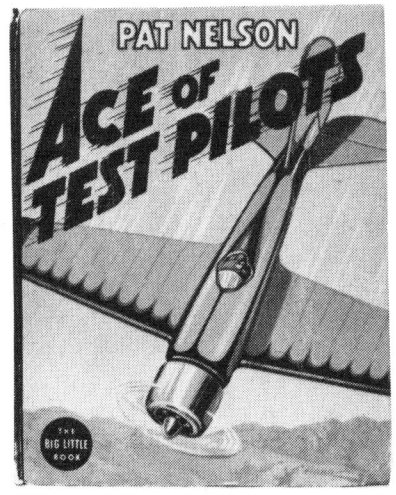

1423 *Peggy Brown and the Secret Treasure.* Kathryn Heisenfelt, Henry Vallely art, 1947.
$7 $11 $15

1491 *Peggy Brown in the Big Haunted House.* Kathryn Heisenfelt, Henry Vallely art, 1940.
$8 $12 $17

1199 *Perry Winkle and the Rinkeydinks.* Martin Branner, 1936.
$7 $11 $15

1487 *Perry Winkle and the Rinkeydinks Get a Horse.* Martin Branner, 1938.
$7 $11 $15

1100 *Phantom, The.* Lee Falk and Ray Moore, first Phantom BLB, 1936.
$14 $23 $30

1421 *Phantom and Desert Justice, The.* Lee Falk and Ray Moore, FM, 1941.
$12 $18 $25

1416 *Phantom and the Girl of Mystery, The.* Lee Falk and Ray Moore, 1947.
$10 $14 $20

1474 *Phantom and the Sign of the Skull, The.* Lee Falk and Ray Moore, 1939.
$13 $21 $29

1468 *Phantom and the Sky Pirates, The.* Lee Falk and Ray Moore, 1945.
$10 $14 $20

1489 *Phantom, The Return of the.* Lee Falk and Ray Moore, left-handed FM, 1942
$12 $18 $25

1466 *Pilot Pete Dive Bomber.* Gaylord DuBois, Robert L. Jenney art, FM, 1941.
$5 $9 $11

1435 *Pinocchio (and Jiminy Cricket).* Walt Disney Studios, based on cartoon, 1940.
$14 $23 $30

1123 *Plainsman, The.* Eleanor Packer, Paramount movie with Gary Cooper, 1936.
$7 $11 $15

1467 *Pluto the Pup.* Walt Disney Studios, 1938.
$12 $18 $25

1497 *Popeye and Castor Oyl the Detective.* Bud Sagandorf, FM, 1941.
$12 $18 $25

1458 *Popeye and Queen Olive Oyl.* Bud Sagandorf, 1949.
$10 $14 $20

1499 *Popeye and the Deep Sea Mystery.* Elzie C. Segar, 1939.
$14 $23 $30

1405 *Popeye and the Jeep.* Elzie C. Segar, 1937.
$14 $23 $30

1459 *Popeye and the Quest for the Rainbird.* Bud Sagandorf, 1943.
$14 $23 $30

1485 *Popeye in a Sock for Susan's Sake.* Elzie C. Segar, FM, 1940.
$12 $18 $25

1450 *Popeye in Quest of His Poopdeck Pappy.* Elzie C. Segar, 1937.
$14 $23 $30

1163 *Popeye Sees the Sea.* Elzie C. Segar, first Popeye BLB (for Whitman), 1936.
$17 $27 $36

1422 *Popeye the Sailor Man.* Bud Sagandorf, all-pix, 1947.
$12 $18 $25

1480 *Popeye the Spinach Eater.* Bud Sagandorf, all-pix, 1945.
$12 $18 $25

1406 *Popeye the Superfighter.* Bud Sagandorf, all-pix, two FMs, 1942.
$12 $18 $25

1404 *Porky Pig and His Gang.* Warner Brothers, two all-pix stories, 1946.
$10 $14 $20

1408 *Porky Pig and Petunia.* Leon Schlesinger Productions, all-pix, two FMs, 1942.
$12 $18 $25

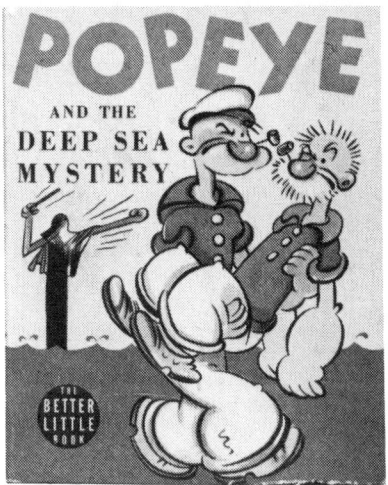

1176 *Powder Smoke Range.* RKO movie with Hoot Gibson and Harey Carey, adapted from William Colt McDonald, 1935.

$7 $11 $15

758 *Prairie Bill and the Covered Wagon.* G.A. Alkire, Hal Arbo cover and art, 1934.

$5 $9 $11

nn *Prairie Bill and the Covered Wagon.* As above, except sc with a different three-color cover illustration, 1934.

$12 $18 $25

1440 *Punch Davis of the Aircraft Carrier.* Roy Snell, J.R. White art, 1945.

$5 $9 $11

1142 *Radio Patrol.* Charles Schmidt sty, Eddie Sullivan art, 1935.

$7 $11 $15

1498 *Radio Patrol and Big Dan's Mobsters.* Charles Schmidt and Eddie Sullivan, 1940.

$7 $11 $15

1496 *Radio Patrol Outwitting the Gang Chief.* Charles Schmidt and Eddie Sullivan, 1939.

$7 $11 $15

1173 *Radio Patrol Trailing the Safeblowers.* Charles Schmidt and Eddie Sullivan, 1937.

$7 $11 $15

1441 *Range Busters in Saddle Mountain Roundup.* Eleanor Packer, Henry Vallely art, adapted from MGM movie, left-handed FM, 1942.

$7 $11 $15

1447 *Ray Land of the Tank Corps U.S.A.* Russell R. Winterbotham, Erwin L. Hess art, cover by Robert Weisman, FM, 1942.

$7 $11 $15

1157 *Red Barry, Hero of the Hour.* Will Gould, excellent example of Will Gould's stylish art, 1935.

$8 $12 $17

1426 Red Barry, Undercover Man. Will Gould, 1939.
$6 $9 $13

1449 Red Death on the Range (A Bronc Peeler Western). Fred Harman, 1940.
$7 $11 $15

1466 Red Ryder and Circus Luck. Fred Harman, 1949.
$6 $9 $13

1400 Red Ryder and Little Beaver on Hoofs of Thunder. Fred Harman, first Red Ryder BLB, 1939.
$12 $18 $25

1400 Red Ryder and Little Beaver on Hoofs of Thunder. As above, except a small pressrun of upside-down covers, 1939.
$14 $20 $29

1427 Red Ryder and the Code of the West. Fred Harman, FM, 1941.
$10 $14 $20

1475 Red Ryder and the Outlaw of Painted Valley. Fred Harman, 1943.
$7 $11 $15

1443 Red Ryder and the Rimrock Killer. Fred Harman, 1948.
$6 $9 $13

1454 Red Ryder and the Secret Canyon. Fred Harman, 1948.
$6 $9 $13

1414 Red Ryder and the Squaw-Tooth Rustlers. Fred Harman, 1946.
$7 $11 $15

1450 Red Ryder and the Western Border Guns. Fred Harman, left-handed FM, 1942.
$8 $13 $18

1473 Red Ryder in War on the Range. Fred Harman, 1945.
$7 $11 $15

1440 Red Ryder, The Fighting Westerner. Fred Harman, 1940.
$8 $13 $18

754 Reg'lar Fellers. Gerne Byrnes, 1933.
$7 $11 $15

1425 *Riders of Lone Trails.* Steve Saxton, 1937.
$5 $9 $11

719 *Robinson Crusoe.* From Daniel DeFoe, sc, round corners, page edges stained red, all-pix, three-color cover, 1933.
$10 $14 $20

1437 *Roy Rogers and the Deadly Treasure.* 1947.
$7 $11 $15

1421 *Roy Rogers and the Dwarf Cattle Ranch.* Don Middleton, Henry Vallely art, 1949.
$8 $13 $18

1448 *Roy Rogers and the Mystery of the Howling Mesa.* 1948.
$7 $11 $15

1462 *Roy Rogers and the Mystery of the Lazy M.* 1949.
$7 $11 $15

1492 *Roy Rogers at Crossed Feathers Ranch.* H.C. Thomas, Erwin L. Hess art, 1945.
$8 $12 $17

1452 *Roy Rogers in Robbers' Roost.* 1948.
$7 $11 $15

1476 *Roy Rogers, King of the Cowboys.* Elizabeth Beecher, Irwin Meyers art, 1943.
$8 $13 $18

1460 *Roy Rogers, Robinhood of the Range.* Edward I. Gruskin, Erwin Hess art, first Roy Rogers BLB, FM, 1942.
$10 $16 $23

1122 (O) *Scrappy.* Pat Patterson, from Columbia cartoon, sc spine, 1934.
$17 $27 $36

1144 *Secret Agent X-9.* Charles Flanders, Alex Raymond art, 1936.
$10 $20 $30

1472 *Secret Agent X-9 and the Mad Assassin.* Robert Storm, Alex Raymond art, 1938.
$8 $12 $18

1161 (O) *Sequoia.* Eleanor Packer, MGM movie with Jean Parker, both hc and sc spines, 1935.
$10 $14 $20

1495 *Shadow and the Ghost Makers, The.* Maxwell Grant, Erwin L. Darwin (really Erwin Hess) art, based on radio program and pulp magazine, FM, John Coleman Burroughs cover, 1942.
$10 $14 $20

1430 *Shadow and the Living Death, The.* Maxwell Grant, Erwin Hess art, 1940.
$10 $18 $25

1443 *Shadow and the Master of Evil, The.* Maxwell Grant, Erwin Hess art, FM, 1941.
$10 $14 $20

1195 *Shooting Sheriffs (Sheriffs of the Wild West).* Leon Morgan, 1936.
$5 $9 $11

1111 *Silly Symphonies Stories, Mickey Mouse Presents Walt Disney's.* Walt Disney Studios, first appearance of Donald Duck in BLB, very scarce, 1936.
$25 $40 $60

1169 *Silly Symphony Featuring Donald Duck.* Al Taliaferro, 1937.
$15 $25 $38

1441 *Silly Symphony Featuring Donald Duck and His (Mis)Adventures.* Al Taliaferro, 1937.
$12 $18 $25

756 (O) *Silly Symphony, Mickey Mouse Presents a.* Walt Disney Studios, scarce, 1934.
$20 $30 $45

1155 (O) *Silver Streak.* Eleanor Packer, RKO movie with Charles Starrett, 1935.
$15 $20 $30

1408 *Skeezix at the Military Academy.* Frank King, 1938.
$5 $9 $11

1414 *Skeezix Goes to War.* Frank King, 1944.
$7 $11 $15

1112 *Skeezix in Africa.* Frank King, 1934.
$8 $13 $18

1419 *Skeezix on His Own in the Big City.* Frank King, all-pix, two FMs, 1941.
$8 $12 $17

761 *Skippy, Story of.* Percy Crosby, Sunday reprints, 1934.
$7 $11 $15

1439 *Skyroads with Clipper Williams of the Flying Legion.* Dick Calkins and Russell Keaton, 1938.
$5 $9 $11

1127 *Skyroads with Hurricane Hawk.* Dick Calkins and Russell Keaton, 1936.
$6 $10 $13

1464 *Smilin' Jack and the Coral Princess.* Zack Mosley, 1938.
$7 $11 $15

1445 *Smilin' Jack and the Escape from Death Rock.* Zack Mosley, 1947.
$7 $11 $15

1419 *Smilin' Jack and the Jungle Pipe Line.* Zack Mosley art, Helen Berke sty, 1946.
$7 $11 $15

1152 *Smilin' Jack and the Stratosphere Ascent.* Zack Mosley, 1937.
$12 $18 $25

1412 *Smilin' Jack Flying High with Downwind.* Zack Mosley, FM, 1942.
$10 $14 $20

1416 *Smilin' Jack in Wings Over the Pacific.* Zack Mosley, 1939.
$10 $14 $20

1473 *Smilin' Jack Speed Pilot.* Zack Mosley, FM, 1941.
$9 $13 $19

1404 *Smitty and Herby Lost Among the Indians.* Walter Berndt, all-pix, two FMs, 1941.
$7 $11 $15

745 *Smitty, Golden Gloves Tournament.* Walter Berndt, 1934.
$9 $13 $19

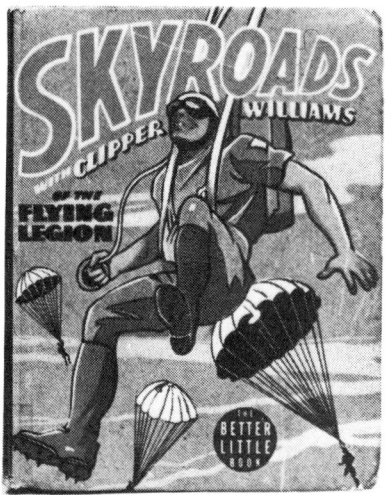
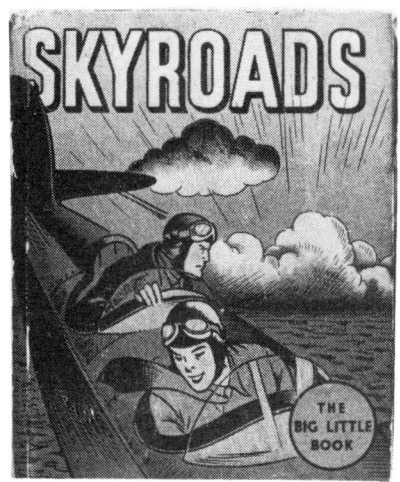

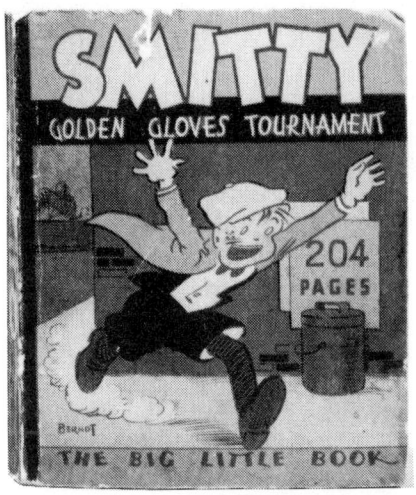

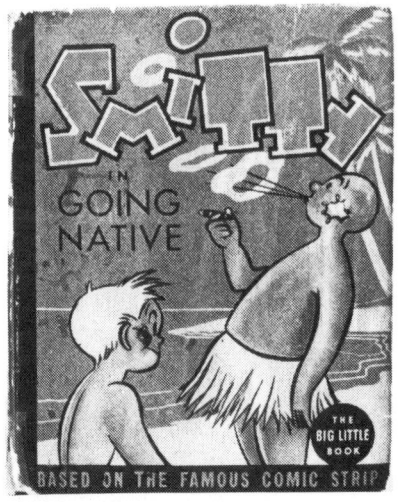

1477 *Smitty in Going Native.* Walter Berndt, 1938.

       $9 $13 $19

1477 *Smitty in Going Native.* As above, except a transition book with BLB logo blacked out, 1938.

       $10 $14 $20

1413 *Smokey Stover, The False Alarm Fireman.* Bill Holman, all-pix, two FMs, 1942.

       $9 $13 $19

1421 *Smokey Stover, The Foo Fighter.* Bill Holman, 1938.

       $10 $18 $25

1481 *Smokey Stover, The Foolish Foo Fighter.* Bill Holman, all-pix, 1945.

       $7 $10 $15

1460 *Snow White and the Seven Dwarfs.* Walt Disney Studios, based on the cartoon, 1938.

       $12 $18 $25

1136 *Sombrero Pete.* Morton H. Cowen, 1936.

       $5 $9 $11

1191 *SOS Coast Guard.* William Engle, Henry Vallely art, 1936.

       $6 $10 $13

1455 *Speed Douglas and the Mole Gang.* Charles Arthur, Erwin L. Hess art, FM, 1941.

       $7 $11 $15

1467 *Spike Kelly of the Commandos.* Art Elder, J.R. White art, 1943.

       $5 $9 $11

768 *Spy, The.* Adapted from Robert Louis Stevenson, 1936.

       $7 $11 $15

1426 *Steve Hunter of the U.S. Coast Guard under Secret Orders.* W.A. Lee, Erwin L. Darwin (really Erwin Hess) art, FM, 1942.

       $5 $9 $11

1149 *Sybil Jason in Little Big Shot.* From Warner Brothers movie, 1935.

       $7 $11 $15

1423 *Tailspin Tommy and the Hooded Flyer.* Hal Forrest, 1937.
$10 $14 $20

1110 *Tailspin Tommy and the Island in the Sky.* Hal Forrest, 1936.
$10 $14 $20

1413 *Tailspin Tommy and the Lost Transport.* Hal Forrest, 1939.
$9 $13 $19

1494 *Tailspin Tommy and the Sky Bandits.* Hal Forrest, scarce, 1938.
$12 $18 $25

1494 *Tailspin Tommy and the Sky Bandits.* As above, except a transition book, BLB logo blacked out, 1938.
$10 $14 $20

1172 *Tailspin Tommy Hunting for Pirate Gold.* Hal Forrest, 1935.
$10 $14 $20

747 *Tailspin Tommy in the Famous Payroll Mystery.* Hal Forrest, first Tailspin Tommy BLB, 1933.
$10 $18 $25

1184 *Tailspin Tommy in the Great Air Mystery.* Hal Forrest, from Universal serial starring Clark Williams and Noah Beery, 1936.
$7 $11 $15

1124 *Tailspin Tommy, The Dirigible Flight to the North Pole.* Hal Forrest, 1934.
$12 $18 $25

nn *Tailspin Tommy, The Dirigible Flight to the North Pole.* As above, except sc with a different three-color cover illustration, 1934.
$17 $27 $36

1410 *Tailspin Tommy, The Weasel and His Skywaymen.* Hal Forrest, all-pix, two FMs, 1941.
$7 $11 $15

1444 *Tarzan and the Ant Men.* Edgar Rice Burroughs, Rex Maxon art, John Coleman Burroughs cover, 1945.
$10 $14 $20

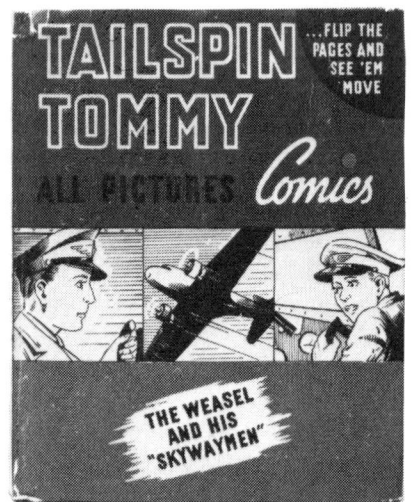

1448 *Tarzan and the Golden Lion.* Edgar Rice Burroughs, Rex Maxon art, John Coleman Burroughs cover, FM, 1943.
$12 $18 $25

1495 *Tarzan and the Jewels of Opar.* Edgar Rice Burroughs, Rex Maxon art, 1940.
$15 $20 $30

1442 *Tarzan and the Lost Empire.* Edgar Rice Burroughs, Rex Maxon art, 1948.
$10 $14 $20

1410 *Tarzan, Beasts of.* Edgar Rice Burroughs, Rex Maxon art, 1937.
$10 $14 $20

1182 *Tarzan Escapes.* Edgar Rice Burroughs, MGM movie with Johnny Weissmuller, 1936.
$7 $11 $15

1467 *Tarzan in the Land of the Giant Apes.* Edgar Rice Burroughs, Jesse Marsh art, from Dell comic book 134, 1949.
$10 $14 $20

1407 *Tarzan, Lord of the Jungle.* Edgar Rice Burroughs, Rex Maxon art, 1946.
$10 $14 $20

1180 (O) *Tarzan, New Adventures of.* Edgar Rice Burroughs, Burroughs-Tarzan Enterprises movie starring Herman Brix, both hc and sc spines, 1935.
$15 $22 $30

744 *Tarzan of the Apes.* Edgar Rice Burroughs, redrawn from Hal Foster strip, first Tarzan BLB, picture and text (underneath) on every page, 1933.
$20 $30 $40

778 *Tarzan of the Screen.* Eleanor Packer, MGM scenes from *Tarzan the Ape Man* and *Tarzan and His Mate*, with Johnny Weissmuller and Maureen O'Sullivan, 1934.
$9 $13 $19

1102 *Tarzan, Return of.* Edgar Rice Burroughs, Rex Maxon art, 1936.
$10 $14 $20

1477 *Tarzan, Son of.* Edgar Rice Burroughs, Rex Maxon art, 1939.
$15 $22 $30

769 *Tarzan the Fearless.* Edgar Rice Burroughs, Principal Pictures serial scenes with Buster Crabbe, 1934.
$10 $14 $20

1453 *Tarzan the Terrible.* Edgar Rice Burroughs, Rex Maxon art, John Coleman Burroughs cover, FM, 1942.
$12 $18 $25

1452 *Tarzan the Untamed.* Edgar Rice Burroughs, Rex Maxon art, John Coleman Burroughs cover, FM, 1941.
$12 $18 $25

770 *Tarzan Twins, The.* Edgar Rice Burroughs, Hal Arbo cover, 1934.
$15 $20 $30

nn *Tarzan Twins, The.* As above, except sc with a different three-color cover illustration, 1934.
$20 $30 $40

770 *Tarzan Twins, The.* Identical to the first 770, except a different copyright date, 1935.
$12 $18 $25

1488 *Tarzan's Revenge.* Edgar Rice Burroughs, movie based, scarce, 1938.
$12 $18 $25

1488 *Tarzan's Revenge.* As above, except a transition book, BLB logo blacked out, 1938.
$10 $14 $20

1156 *Terry and the Pirates.* Milton Caniff, first Terry BLB, 1935.
$12 $18 $25

1446 *Terry and the Pirates and the Giant's Vengeance.* Milton Caniff, 1939.
$10 $14 $20

1499 *Terry and the Pirates in the Mountain Stronghold.* Milton Caniff, 1941.
$9 $13 $19

1412 *Terry and the Pirates Shipwrecked on a Desert Island*. Milton Caniff, 1938.
$8 $13 $18

1436 *Terry and the Pirates, The Plantation Mystery*. Milton Caniff, FM, 1942.
$9 $13 $19

1420 *Terry and War in the Jungle*. Helen Berke, Milton Caniff art, 1946.
$7 $11 $15

1492 *Terry Lee, Flight Officer U.S.A.* Milton Caniff, 1944, reprint of classic Terry strip from October, 1942—featured in Coulton Waugh's *The Comics*, 1947, p. 273.
$10 $14 $20

1440 *Tex Thorne Comes Out of the West*. Zane Grey, beautiful Allen Dean art, Hal Arbo cover, 1937.
$8 $13 $18

1429 *Texas Kid, The*. Steve Saxton, Milt Youngren art, 1937.
$5 $9 $11

1135 *Texas Ranger on the Trail of the Dog Town Rustlers*. Leon Morgan, Hal Arbo art, 1936.
$5 $9 $11

1131 (O) *Three Musketeers, The*. John Adams, a Feature Movie Book® produced under the BLB 1100 series, RKO movie starring Walter Abel, sc, 1935.
$15 $20 $27

1409 *Thumper and the Seven Dwarfs*. Walt Disney Studios, all-pix, 1944.
$10 $14 $20

1442 *Tillie the Toiler and the Wild Man of Desert Island*. Russ Westover, FM, 1941.
$9 $13 $19

1490 *Tim McCoy and the Sandy Gulch Stampede*. Gaylord DuBois, 1939.
$7 $11 $15

1152 (O) *Tim McCoy in the Prescott Kid*. Eleanor Packer, from Columbia movie, sc spine, 1935.
$10 $14 $20

1193 *Tim McCoy in the Westerner.* Eleanor Packer, from Columbia movie, 1936.
$7 $11 $15

1436 *Tim McCoy on the Tomahawk Trail.* Gaylord DuBois, 1937.
$7 $11 $15

1140 *Tim Tyler's Luck, Adventures in the Ivory Patrol.* Lyman Young, 1937.
$8 $13 $18

1479 *Tim Tyler's Luck and the Plot of the Exiled King.* Lyman Young, possible Alex Raymond assist, 1939.
$8 $13 $18

767 *Tiny Tim, The Adventures of.* Stanley Link, art and sty suspiciously similar to Calkins and Yager of Buck Rogers fame, possible assist, 1935.
$9 $13 $19

1472 *Tiny Tim and the Big, Big World.* Stanley Link, 1945.
$7 $11 $15

1172 *Tiny Tim and the Mechanical Men.* Stanley Link, 1937.
$9 $13 $19

723 (O) *Tom Beatty, Ace of the Service.* Richard X. Vale, George R. Taylor art, 1934.
$10 $14 $20

nn (O) *Tom Beatty, Ace of the Service.* As above, except sc with a different three-color cover illustration, 1934.
$15 $22 $30

1420 *Tom Beatty, Ace of the Service, and the Big Brain Gang.* Rex Loomis, William Mark Young art, 1939.
$5 $9 $11

1165 *Tom Beatty, Ace of the Service, Scores Again.* Russell R. Winterbotham, Robert Weisman art, 1937.
$7 $11 $15

1482 *Tom Mix and His Circus on the Barbary Coast.* Pete Daryll, James Gary art, 1940.
$7 $11 $15

1462 *Tom Mix and the Hoard of Montezuma.* Wilton West, Henry Vallely art, 1937.
$7 $11 $15

1183 *Tom Mix and the Stranger from the South.* Pete Daryll, from movie but no photos, 1936.
$7 $11 $15

762 (O) *Tom Mix and Tony, Jr. in Terror Trail.* Universal movie, first Tom Mix BLB, hc with sc spine, 1935.
$22 $35 $47

1144 *Tom Mix in the Fighting Cowboy.* Leon Morgan, Hal Arbo art, 1935.
$10 $14 $20

nn *Tom Mix in the Fighting Cowboy.* As above, except sc with a different three-color cover illustration, 1935.
$15 $22 $30

1166 *Tom Mix in the Range War.* Buck Wilson, Hal Arbo art, 1937.
$7 $11 $15

1173 (O) *Tom Mix Plays a Lone Hand.* Wilton West, Hal Arbo art, hc with sc spine, 1935.
$10 $14 $20

1485 *Tom Swift and His Giant Telescope.* Victor Appleton, James Gary art, 1939.
$7 $11 $15

1437 *Tom Swift and His Magnetic Silencer.* Victor Appleton, J.R. White art, FM, 1941.
$10 $14 $20

720 *Treasure Island.* Adapted from Robert Louis Stevenson, all-pix, sc, round corners, page edges stained purple, Juanita Bennett art, 1933.
$12 $18 $25

1141 (O) *Treasure Island.* Eleanor Packer, MGM movie with Jackie Cooper, hc with sc spine, 1934.
$10 $14 $20

1104 *Two-Gun Montana.* Tex Reynolds, Henry Vallely art, 1936.
$6 $10 $13

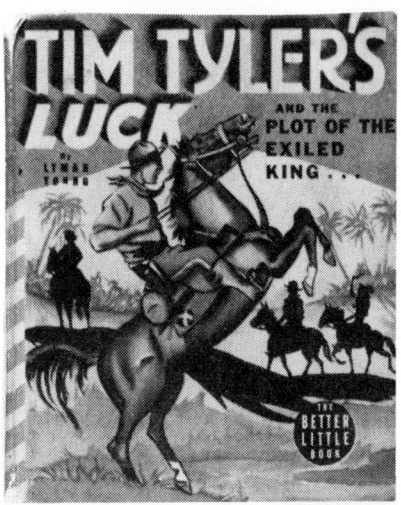

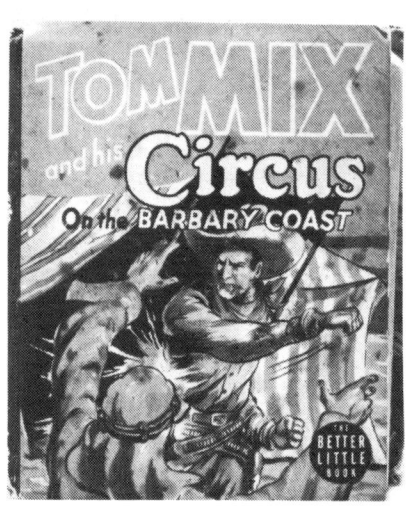

1114 *Uncle Don's Strange Adventures.* Uncle Don Carney, from radio program, 1936.
$6 $10 $13

722 *Uncle Ray's Story of the United States.* Ramon Coffman, 1934.
$5 $9 $11

1461 *Uncle Sam's Sky Defenders.* Peter A. Wyckoff, Erwin L. Hess art, FM, 1941.
$7 $11 $15

1405 *Uncle Wiggily's Adventures.* Howard R. Garis, all-pix, 1946.
$7 $11 $15

1411 *Union Pacific.* Eleanor Packer, Paramount movie with Joel McCrea and Barbara Stanwyck, 1939.
$7 $11 $15

1455 *Vic Sands of the U.S. Flying Fortress.* Roy J. Snell, Neil Slocum art, 1943.
$5 $9 $11

1455 *Wash Tubbs and Captain Easy Hunting for Whales.* Roy Crane, 1938.
$7 $11 $15

751 *Wash Tubbs in Pandemonia.* Roy Crane, 1934.
$10 $14 $20

751 *Wash Tubbs in Pandemonia.* As above, except sc, 1934.
$12 $18 $25

1471 *Wells Fargo.* Eleanor Packer, Paramount movie with Bob Burns and Joel McCrea, 1938.
$6 $10 $13

1164 (O) *West Point of the Air.* Eleanor Packer, MGM movie with Wallace Beery and Robert Young, sc spine, 1935.
$10 $14 $20

1458 *Wimpy the Hamburger Eater.* Elzie C. Segar, 1938.
$12 $18 $25

1433 *Windy Wayne and His Flying Wing.* Russell R. Winterbotham, Erwin L. Darwin (really Erwin Hess) art, left-handed FM, 1942.
$5 $9 $11

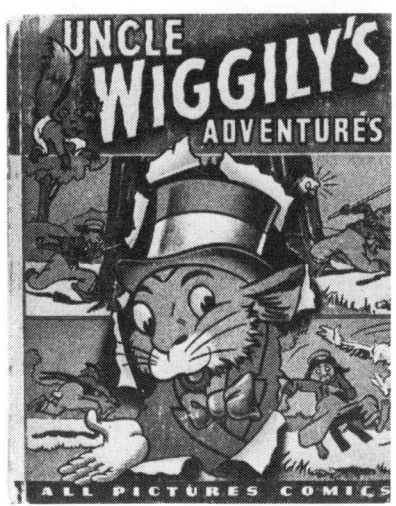

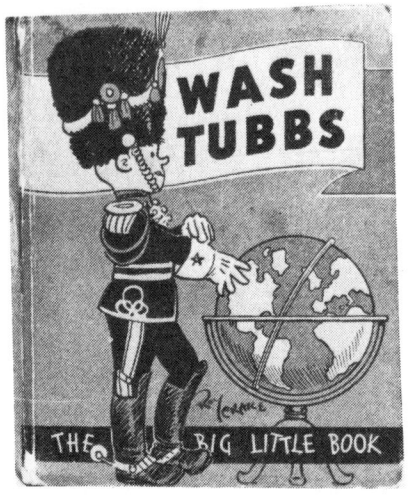

1407 *Wings of the U.S.A.* Peter A. Wyckoff, Thomas Hickey art, 1940.
$5 $9 $11

1108 *Winsie Atkins, Flying the Sky Clipper with.* Dougal Lee, 1936.
$6 $9 $12

779 (O) *World War in Photographs.* Otto Kurth, World War I photos from newsreel scenes, 1934.
$10 $18 $25

1465 *Zip Saunders, King of the Speedway.* Rex Loomis, Robert R. Weisman art, 1939.
$6 $9 $13

New Better Little Books® (1949-1950)

The New Better Little Books®, or the 700-10 series, are hardbound, 200-page books with the dimensions 3⅛ x 5½ x ⅝ inches. Each book has one illustration per page, with text below. These books are also found in many lists as the 700N series because of their "new" tall and narrow format. The New Better Little Books® were produced in four sets: two sets of four titles in 1949 (700-10 to 707-10), one set of four titles in early 1950 (708-10 to 711-10), and one set of three titles in late 1950 (712-10, 714-10, and 715-10). There is no 713-10. The first set of four titles has black and white illustrations; the second set has red added to the drawings. The third set has green in its pictures, and the final three titles have blue. Story lines for most of these books are from the daily comic strips.

707-10 Andy Panda and Presto the Pup. Walter Lantz Productions, red added to illustrations, 1949.
$5 $10 $15

703-10 Blondie and Dagwood, Some Fun! Chic Young, 1949.
$6 $12 $18

704-10 Brer Rabbit. Walt Disney Productions, red added to illustrations, 1949.
$5 $9 $13

706-10 Bugs Bunny and the Giant Brothers. Warner Brothers Productions, red added to illustrations, 1949.
$5 $10 $15

711-10 Cinderella and the Magic Wand. Walt Disney Productions, green added to illustrations, 1950.
$5 $10 $15

705-10 Donald Duck and the Mystery of the Double X. Carl Barks sty and art, red added to illustrations, 1949.
$8 $15 $20

700-10 Gene Autry and the Bandits of Silver Tip. 1949.
$6 $12 $18

714-10 Gene Autry and the Range War. Scarce, blue added to illustrations, 1950.
$9 $16 $23

712-10 Lone Ranger and the Secret of Somber Canyon. Blue added to illustrations, 1950.
$5 $10 $15

708-10 *Mickey Mouse on the Haunted Island.* Floyd Gottfredson sty and art, green added to illustrations, 1950.
$8 $15 $20

702-10 *Red Ryder, Acting Sheriff.* Fred Harman, 1949.
$5 $10 $15

701-10 *Roy Rogers and the Snowbound Outlaws.* 1949.
$5 $10 $15

715-10 *Roy Rogers, Range Detective.* Blue added to illustrations, 1950.
$5 $10 $15

709-10 *Tarzan and the Journey of Terror.* Edgar Rice Burroughs, Jesse Marsh art, from Dell Tarzan comic 7, green added to illustrations, 1950.
$7 $13 $18

710-10 *Woody Woodpecker, Big Game Hunter.* Walter Lantz Productions, green added to illustrations, 1950.
$5 $10 $15

Big Little Book TV Series® (1958)

Eight years after production ceased on the New Better Little Books,® Whitman Publishing Company incorporated into the larger Western Publishing Company and began the Big Little Book TV Series.® This series is based on popular television broadcasts of the time. The books are laminated hardbacks, 280 pages long, and are larger than traditional BLBs. Two colors were added to interior illustrations, each color alternating, generally, every five pages. For example, after five pages of pale yellow, one can look forward to five pages of sickly green. Six titles were produced, all in 1958.

1648 *Adventures of Jim Bowie.* Lewis B. Patten, Tony Sgroi art, 1958.
$5 $10 $15

1645 *Andy Burnett on Trial (Walt Disney's)*. Charles I. Combes, Henry Luhrs art, 1958.
$5 $10 $15

1646 *Buccaneers, The*. Alice Sankey, Russ Manning art, 1958.
$5 $10 $15

1647 *Gunsmoke*. Doris Schroeder, John Ushler art, 1958.
$7 $12 $17

1649 *Sir Lancelot*. Dorothy Haas, Helmuth Wegner art, 1958.
$5 $10 $15

1644 *Wyatt Earp (Hugh O'Brian TV's)*. Davis Lott, John Ushler art, 1958.
$7 $12 $17

A Big Little Book® (1967-1969, 1973-present)

In 1967, Whitman returned to BLB production, this time using the logo A Big Little Book®. There were two distinct series: the 2000 series (published from 1967 to 1969), and the 5700 series (beginning in 1973 and continuing to the present).

The 2000 series introduced thirty-five titles, the first twelve of which had two reprintings each. Because of the confusion these reprint editions have caused, a simple identification description follows: Blue endpapers with repeating white circle and BLB logo indicates first printing (1967); white (plain) endpapers with repeating light-gray circle and BLB logo indicates second printing (early 1968); white (plain) endpapers with no logo indicates third printing (fall, 1968).

Fifteen new titles were released late in 1968, and eight new titles in 1969. These books, 2013-2035, all have plain endpapers with no BLB logo. In all of the above descriptions, it should be noted that reference to the BLB logo concerns the endpapers only. For example, on the third printing, while no logo appears on the endpapers, all of these books have a BLB logo on the spine.

The BLBs of the 2000 series are 256 pages long and contain four-color illustrations opposite a page of text. Though most have a 39-cent price on the cover, some books appear without this price.

The 5700 series was initiated by an agreement in 1973 between Whitman and the K-Mart Corporation to produce twelve cheaply made "limpbound"

BLBs: ten reprints from the 2000 series and two adaptations from earlier BLBs (1457 and 1458). After that, six more titles were made for K-Mart in 1974 followed by nineteen other titles independently produced by Whitman. There are thirty-seven titles, so far, in the 5700 series. There are numerous reprint editions, making a paragraph description of the series all the more confusing. Instead, variation printings will be described title-by-title as they are priced. About the only consistent characteristic of BLBs in the 5700 series is the unusually soft cover. Another is page length—256 pages. Books in the 2000 series are listed first, followed by books in the 5700 series.

2017 *Aquaman, Scourge of the Sea.* Paul S. Newman, 1968.
$2 $4 $5

2031 *Batman and Robin in the Cheetah Caper.* George S. Elrick, 1969.
$2 $4 $5

2023 *Beep Beep, The Road Runner, The Super Beep-Catcher.* Carl Fallberg, with and without 39-cent price on cover, 1968.
$2 $4 $5

2002 *Bonanza, The Bubble Gum Kid.* George S. Elrick, 1967.
$3 $5 $7

2002 *Bonanza, The Bubble Gum Kid.* Second printing, 1968.
$2 $4 $5

2002 *Bonanza, The Bubble Gum Kid.* Third printing, 1968.
$2 $3 $4

2029 *Bugs Bunny, Accidental Adventure.* Don Christensen, Warner Brothers-Seven Arts, 1969.
$2 $4 $5

2007 *Bugs Bunny in Double Trouble on Diamond Island.* Don Christensen, Warner Brothers Productions, 1967.
$3 $5 $7

2007 *Bugs Bunny in Double Trouble on Diamond Island.* Second printing, 1968.
$2 $4 $5

2007 *Bugs Bunny in Double Trouble on Diamond Island.* Third printing, 1968.
$2 $3 $4

2025 *Chitty Chitty Bang Bang.* Adapted from Ian Fleming and the movie by William Johnston, 1968.
$3 $4 $6

2018 *Daktari, Night of Terror, Ivan Tors'.* George S. Elrick, 1968.
$2 $4 $5

2001 *Dick Tracy Encounters Facey.* Paul S. Newman, 1967.
$4 $6 $8

2001 *Dick Tracy Encounters Facey.* Second printing, 1968.
$2 $4 $5

2001 *Dick Tracy Encounters Facey.* Third printing, 1968.
$2 $3 $4

2033 *Donald Duck, Luck of the Ducks, Walt Disney's.* Carl Fallberg, Walt Disney Productions art, 1969.
$2 $4 $5

2009 *Donald Duck, The Fabulous Diamond Fountain, Walt Disney's.* Carl Fallberg, Walt Disney Productions art, 1967.
$3 $5 $7

2009 *Donald Duck, The Fabulous Diamond Fountain, Walt Disney's.* Second printing, 1968.
$2 $4 $5

2009 *Donald Duck, The Fabulous Diamond Fountain, Walt Disney's.* Third printing, 1968.
$2 $3 $4

2019 *Fantastic Four in the House of Horrors, The.* William Johnston, from the Marvel comic book, 1968.
$2 $4 $5

2014 *Flintstones, The Case of the Many Missing Things, Hanna-Barbera's.* Paul S. Newman, 1968.
$2 $4 $5

2032 *Flipper, Deep-Sea Photographer.* George S. Elrick, from Ivan Tors' TV show, with and without 39-cent price on cover, 1969.
$2 $4 $5

2003 *Flipper, Killer Whale Trouble.* George S. Elrick, from Ivan Tors' TV show, 1967.
$3 $5 $7

2003 *Flipper, Killer Whale Trouble.* Second printing, 1968.
$2 $4 $5

2003 *Flipper, Killer Whale Trouble.* Third printing, 1968.
$2 $3 $4

2015 *Frankenstein, Jr., The Menace of the Heartless Monster, Hanna-Barbera's.* Carl Fallberg, 1968.
$2 $4 $5

2035 *Gentle Ben, Mystery in the Everglades, Ivan Tors'.* Paul S. Newman, 1969.
$2 $4 $5

2021 *Goofy in Giant Trouble, Walt Disney's.* Don Christensen, Walt Disney Productions art, with and without 39-cent price on cover, 1968.
$2 $4 $5

2012 *Invaders, Alien Missile Threat.* Paul S. Newman, from TV show created by Larry Cohen, 1967.
$3 $5 $7

2012 *Invaders, Alien Missile Threat.* Second printing, 1968.
$2 $4 $5

2012 *Invaders, Alien Missile Threat.* Third printing, 1968.
$2 $3 $4

2026 *Journey to the Center of the Earth, The Fiery Foe.* Paul S. Newman, 1968.
$2 $4 $5

2004 *Lassie, Adventure in Alaska.* George S. Elrick, 1967.
$3 $5 $7

2004 *Lassie, Adventure in Alaska.* Second printing, 1968.
$2 $4 $5

2004 *Lassie, Adventure in Alaska.* Third printing, 1968.
$2 $3 $4

2027 *Lassie and the Shabby Sheik.* George S. Elrick, 1968.
$2 $4 $5

2013 *Lone Ranger Outwits Crazy Cougar, The.* George S. Elrick, 1968.
$3 $4 $6

2022 *Major Matt Mason, Moon Mission.* George S. Elrick, based on Mattel toy, with and without 39-cent price on cover, 1968.
$2 $4 $5

2011 *Man from U.N.C.L.E., The Calcutta Affair.* George S. Elrick, from the popular TV series, 1967.
$4 $6 $7

2011 *Man from U.N.C.L.E., The Calcutta Affair.* Second printing, 1968.
$2 $4 $6

2011 *Man from U.N.C.L.E., The Calcutta Affair.* Third printing, 1968.
$2 $3 $5

2020 *Mickey Mouse, Adventure in Outer Space, Walt Disney's.* George E. Davie, Floyd Gottfredson art, 1968.
$4 $6 $7

2034 *Popeye, Danger, Ahoy!* Paul S. Newman, 1969.
$3 $4 $6

2008 *Popeye, Ghost Ship to Treasure Island.* Paul S. Newman, 1967.
$4 $6 $7

2008 *Popeye, Ghost Ship to Treasure Island.* Second printing, 1968.
$2 $4 $5

2008 *Popeye, Ghost Ship to Treasure Island.* Third printing, 1968.
$2 $3 $4

2024 *Shazzan, The Glass Princess, Hanna-Barbera's.* Don Christensen, 1968.
$2 $4 $5

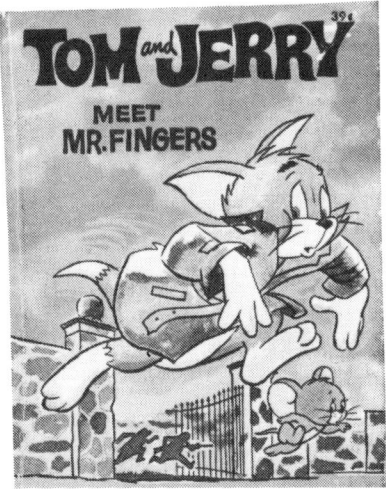

2016 *Space Ghost, The Sorceress of Cyba-3, Hanna-Barbera's*. Don R. Christensen, 1968.
$2 $4 $5

2005 *Tarzan, The Mark of the Red Hyena, Edgar Rice Burroughs'*. George S. Elrick, Jerry Pellini art, 1967.
$4 $6 $7

2005 *Tarzan, The Mark of the Red Hyena, Edgar Rice Burroughs'*. Second printing, 1968.
$3 $5 $7

2005 *Tarzan, The Mark of the Red Hyena, Edgar Rice Burroughs'*. Third printing, 1968.
$2 $3 $5

2006 *Tom and Jerry Meet Mr. Fingers*. Carl Fallberg, 1967.
$3 $5 $7

2006 *Tom and Jerry Meet Mr. Fingers*. Second printing, 1968.
$2 $4 $5

2006 *Tom and Jerry Meet Mr. Fingers*. Third printing, 1968.
$2 $3 $4

2030 *Tom and Jerry, The Astro-Nots, MGM's*. William Johnston, with and without 39-cent price on cover, 1969.
$2 $4 $5

2010 *Woody Woodpecker and the Meteor Menace, Walter Lantz'*. Don R. Christensen, Walter Lantz Productions art, 1967.
$3 $5 $7

2010 *Woody Woodpecker and the Meteor Menace, Walter Lantz'*. Second printing, 1968.
$2 $4 $5

2010 *Woody Woodpecker and the Meteor Menace, Walter Lantz'*. Third printing, 1968.
$2 $3 $4

2028 *Woody Woodpecker, The Sinister Signal, Walter Lantz'*. Vic Lockman, Walter Lantz Productions art, 1969.
$2 $4 $5

5771 *Batman, The Cheetah Caper.* George S. Elrick, reissue of 2031 minus color pix, 49-cent cover price, 1975.

              $1   under $1 $2

5771 *Batman, The Cheetah Caper.* Identical to above, except a 69-cent cover price, 1977-1978.

              under $1 $1

5771-1 *Batman, The Cheetah Caper.* Identical to above, except a different number, 1979.

              under $1 $1

5771-2 *Batman, The Cheetah Caper.* Identical to 5771-1, except a 79-cent cover price and a different number, 1980.

              under $1

5758 *Bugs Bunny, Accidental Adventure.* Don R. Christensen, reissue of 2029, FM, no cover price, 1973.

              under $1 $2

5758 *Bugs Bunny, Accidental Adventure.* Identical to above, except a 39-cent cover price, 1974.

              under $1 $1

5758-1 *Bugs Bunny, Accidental Adventure.* Identical to above, except a 69-cent cover price and a different number, 1979.

              under $1 $1

5766 *Bugs Bunny and Klondike Gold.* Adapted from BLB 1455 with FM added, a BLB classic, no cover price, 1974.

              under $1 $2

5766 *Bugs Bunny and Klondike Gold.* Identical to above, except a 39-cent cover price, 1974.

              under $1 $1

5766 *Bugs Bunny and Klondike Gold.* Identical to above, except a 49-cent cover price, 1975.

              under $1 $1

5766 *Bugs Bunny and Klondike Gold.* Identical to above, except a 69-cent cover price, 1977-1978.

              under $1 $1

5766-1 *Bugs Bunny and Klondike Gold.* Identical to above, except a different number, 1979.

              under $1 $1

5766-2 *Bugs Bunny and Klondike Gold.* Identical to 5766-1, except a 79-cent cover price and a different number, 1980.

              under $1 $1

5757 *Bugs Bunny in Double Trouble on Diamond Island.* Don R. Christensen, four-color illustration, no cover price, 1973.

              $2 $3 $4

5757 *Bugs Bunny in Double Trouble on Diamond Island.* Identical to above, except a 39-cent cover price, 1974.

              $1 $2 $3

5757-1 *Bugs Bunny in Double Trouble on Diamond Island.* Identical to above, except black and white pix and a different number, 1979.

              under $1 $1

5757-2 *Bugs Bunny in Double Trouble on Diamond Island.* Identical to 5757-1, except a 79-cent cover price and a different number, 1980.

under $1 $1

5772 *Bugs Bunny the Last Crusader.* Rita Ritchie, FM, 49-cent cover price, 1975.

under $1 $1 $2

5772 *Bugs Bunny the Last Crusader.* Identical to above, except a 49-cent cover price, 1977-1978.

under $1 $1

5772-1 *Bugs Bunny the Last Crusader.* Identical to above, except a different number, 1979.

under $1 $1

5772-2 *Bugs Bunny the Last Crusader.* Identical to 5772-1, except a 79-cent cover price and a different number, 1980.

under $1 $1

5785-2 *Daffy Duck in Twice the Trouble.* Don Christensen, 79-cent cover price, 1980.

under $1 $1

5760 *Donald Duck in Volcano Valley.* Adapted from BLB 1457 with FM from 1424 added, a BLB classic, no cover price, 1973.

$1 $2 $3

5760 *Donald Duck in Volcano Valley.* Identical to above, except a 39-cent cover price, 1974.

$1 $2 $3

5760-1 *Donald Duck in Volcano Valley.* Identical to above, except a 69-cent cover price and a different number, 1979.

under $1 $1

5760-2 *Donald Duck in Volcano Valley.* Identical to above, except a 79-cent cover price and a different number, 1980.

under $1 $1

5764 *Donald Duck, Luck of the Ducks, Walt Disney's.* Carl Fallberg, reissue of 2033, no cover price, four-color illustration, 1974.

$1 $2 $3

5764 *Donald Duck, Luck of the Ducks, Walt Disney's.* Identical to above, except a 39-cover price, 1974.

$1 $2 $3

5764 *Donald Duck, Luck of the Ducks, Walt Disney's.* Identical to above, except a 49-cent cover price and black and white pix, 1975.

under $1 $1

5764-1 *Donald Duck, Luck of the Ducks, Walt Disney's.* Identical to above, except a 69-cent cover price and a different number, 1979.

under $1 $1

5756 *Donald Duck, The Fabulous Diamond Fountain, Walt Disney's.* Carl Fallberg, four-color illustration, no cover price, reissue of 2009, 1973.

$2 $3 $4

5756 *Donald Duck, The Fabulous Diamond Fountain, Walt Disney's.* Identical to above, except a 39-cent cover price, 1974.

$1 $2 $3

5756-1 *Donald Duck, The Fabulous Diamond Fountain, Walt Disney's.* Identical to above, except a 69-cent cover price, black and white pix, and a different number, 1979.

under $1 $1

5756-2 *Donald Duck, The Fabulous Diamond Fountain, Walt Disney's.* Identical to 5756-1, except a 79-cent cover price and a different number, 1980.

under $1 $1

5773 *Donald Duck, The Lost Jungle City, Walt Disney's.* FM, 49-cent cover price, 1975.

under $1.50 $2

5773 *Donald Duck, The Lost Jungle City, Walt Disney's.* Identical to above, except a 69-cent cover price, 1977-1978.

under $1 $1

5773-1 *Donald Duck, The Lost Jungle City, Walt Disney's.* Identical to above, except a different number, 1979.

under $1 $1

5773-2 *Donald Duck, The Lost Jungle City, Walt Disney's.* Identical to above, except a 79-cent cover price and a different number, 1980.

                        under $1   **$1**

5775 *Fantastic Four in the House of Horrors.* William Johnston, reissue of 2019, 49-cent cover price, 1976.

                        under $1   **$1**

5775-1 *Fantastic Four in the House of Horrors.* Identical to above, except a 69-cent cover price and a different number, 1979.

                        under $1   **$1**

5751 *Goofy in Giant Trouble, Walt Disney's.* Don R. Christensen, reissue of 2021, four-color illustration, no cover price, 1973.

                        $2   **$3**   **$4**

5751 *Goofy in Giant Trouble, Walt Disney's.* Identical to above, except a 39-cent cover price, 1974.

                        $2   **$3**   **$4**

5751 *Goofy in Giant Trouble, Walt Disney's.* Identical to above, except black and white pix and a 69-cent cover price, 1977-1978.

                        under $1   **$1**

5751-1 *Goofy in Giant Trouble, Walt Disney's.* Identical to above, except a different number, 1979.

                        under $1   **$1**

5751-2 *Goofy in Giant Trouble, Walt Disney's.* Identical to 5751-1, except a different number, 1980.

                        under $1   **$1**

5778 *Grimm's Ghost Stories.* Retold by Laura French, 49-cent cover price, 1976.

                        under $1.50   **$2**

5778-1 *Grimm's Ghost Stories.* Identical to 5778, except a 69-cent cover price and a different number, 1979.

                        under $1   **$1**

5782-2 *Incredible Hulk, Lost in Time, The.* Don Glut, 79-cent cover price, 1980.

                        under $1   **$1**

5754 *Lassie, Adventure in Alaska.* George S. Elrick, reissue of 2004, no cover price, four-color illustration, 1973.

                        $2   **$3**   **$4**

5754 *Lassie, Adventure in Alaska.* Identical to above, except a 39-cent cover price, 1974.

                        $2   **$3**   **$4**

5754-1 *Lassie, Adventure in Alaska.* Identical to above, except a 69-cent cover price and a different number, black and white pix, 1979.

                        under $1   **$1**

5762 *Lassie and the Shabby Sheik.* George S. Elrick, reissue of 2027, four-color illustration, no cover price, 1974.

                        $2   **$3**   **$4**

5762 *Lassie and the Shabby Sheik.* Identical to above, except a 39-cent cover price, 1974.

                        $2   **$3**   **$4**

5762-1 *Lassie and the Shabby Sheik.* Identical to above, except black and white pix, 69-cent cover price and a different number, 1979.

                        under $1   **$1**

5769 *Lassie, Old One Eye.* George S. Elrick, 49-cent cover price, 1975.

                        under $1   **$1**   **$2**

5769-1 *Lassie, Old One Eye.* Identical to 5769, except a 69-cent cover price and different number, 1979.
under $1

5774 *Lone Ranger Outwits Crazy Cougar, The.* George S. Elrick, reissue of 2013, 49-cent cover price, 1976.
under $1 **$1**

5774-1 *Lone Ranger Outwits Crazy Cougar, The.* Identical to 5774, except a 69-cent cover price and a different number, 1979.
under $1

5750 *Mickey Mouse, Adventure in Outer Space, Walt Disney's.* George E. Davie, reissue of 2020, four-color illustration, no cover price, 1973.
$2 **$3** **$4**

5750 *Mickey Mouse, Adventure in Outer Space, Walt Disney's.* Identical to above, except a 39-cent cover price, 1974.
$2 **$3** **$4**

5750-1 *Mickey Mouse, Adventure in Outer Space, Walt Disney's.* Identical to above, except black and white pix, 69-cent cover price and a different number, 1979.
under $1

5781-2 *Mickey Mouse, Mystery at Dead Man's Cove, Walt Disney's.* 79-cent cover price, 1980.
under $1

5770 *Mickey Mouse, Mystery at Disneyland, Walt Disney's.* 49-cent cover price, 1975.
under $1.50 **$2**

5770 *Mickey Mouse, Mystery at Disneyland, Walt Disney's.* Identical to above, except a 69-cent cover price, 1977-1978.
under $1 **$1**

5770-1 *Mickey Mouse, Mystery at Disneyland, Walt Disney's.* Identical to above, except a different number, 1979.
under $1 **$1**

5770-2 *Mickey Mouse, Mystery at Disneyland, Walt Disney's.* Identical to 5770-1, except a 79-cent cover price and a different number, 1980.
under $1

5776 *Pink Panther, Adventures in Z-Land.* David L. Harrison, FM, 49-cent cover price, 1976.
under $1.50 **$2**

5776 *Pink Panther, Adventures in Z-Land.* Identical to above, except a 69-cent cover price, 1977-1978.
under $1 **$1**

5776-1 *Pink Panther, Adventures in Z-Land.* Identical to above, except a different number, 1979.
under $1

5776-2 *Pink Panther, Adventures in Z-Land.* Identical to 5776-1, except a 79-cent cover price and a different number, 1980.
under $1

5783-2 *Pink Panther, At Castle Kreep.* Don Glut, 79-cent cover price, 1980.
under $1

5761 *Popeye and Queen Olive Oyl.* Adapted from BLB 1458 with FM from 1497 added, a BLB classic, no cover price, 1973.
$1 **$2** **$3**

5761 *Popeye and Queen Olive Oyl.* Identical to above, except a 39-cent cover price, 1974.
under $1.25 **$2**

5761-1 *Popeye and Queen Olive Oyl.* Identical to above, except a 69-cent cover price and a different number, 1979.
under $1 **$1**

5761-2 *Popeye and Queen Olive Oyl.* Identical to 5761-1, except a 79-cent cover price and a different number, 1980.
under $1

5768 *Popeye, Danger Ahoy!* Paul S. Newman, reissue of 2034, 49-cent cover price, 1975.
under $1.25 **$2**

5768 *Popeye, Danger Ahoy!* Identical to above, except a 69-cent cover price, 1979.

under $1 $1

5755 *Popeye, Ghost Ship to Treasure Island.* Paul S. Newman, reissue of 2008, four-color illustration, no cover price, 1973.

$2 $3 $4

5755 *Popeye, Ghost Ship to Treasure Island.* Identical to above, except a 39-cent cover price, 1974.

$2 $3 $4

5755 *Popeye, Ghost Ship to Treasure Island.* Identical to above, except black and white pix and 49-cent cover price, 1975.

under $1 $1

5755-1 *Popeye, Ghost Ship to Treasure Island.* Identical to above, except a 69-cent cover price and a different number, 1979.

under $1 $1

5786-2 *Popeye in Deep Sea Danger.* Paul S. Newman, 79-cent cover price, 1980.

under $1 $1

5784-2 *Road Runner and the Unidentified Flying Coyote, Beep Beep the.* George S. Elrick, 79-cent cover price, 1980.

under $1 $1

5767 *Road Runner, Beep Beep, The Lost Road Runner Mine.* FM, no cover price, Carl Fallberg sty, 1974.

under $1.50 $2

5767 *Road Runner, Beep Beep, The Lost Road Runner Mine.* Identical to above, except a 39-cent cover price, 1974.

under $1.25 $1

5767 *Road Runner, Beep Beep, The Lost Road Runner Mine.* Identical to above, except a 49-cent cover price, 1975.

under $1 $1

5767 *Road Runner, Beep Beep, The Lost Road Runner Mine.* Identical to above, except a 69-cent cover price, 1977-1978.

under $1 $1

5767-1 *Road Runner, Beep Beep, The Lost Road Runner Mine.* Identical to above, except a different number, 1979.

under $1

5767-2 *Road Runner, Beep Beep, The Lost Road Runner Mine.* Identical to 5767-1, except a 79-cent cover price and a different number, 1980.

under $1

5759 *Road Runner, Beep Beep, The Super Beep-Catcher.* Carl Fallberg, reissue of 2023, FM, no cover price, 1973.

under $1.25 $2

5759 *Road Runner, Beep Beep, The Super Beep-Catcher.* Identical to above, except a 39-cent cover price, 1974.

under $1 $1

5759-1 *Road Runner, Beep Beep, The Super Beep-Catcher.* Identical to above, except a 69-cent cover price and a different number, 1979.

under $1

5779 *Spider-Man Zaps Mr. Zodiac.* George S. Elrick, 49-cent cover price, 1976.

under $1 $1

5779 *Spider-Man Zaps Mr. Zodiac.* Identical to above, except a 69-cent cover price, 1977-1978.

under $1

5779-2 *Spider-Man Zaps Mr. Zodiac.* Identical to above, except a 79-cent cover price and a different number, 1980.

under $1

5752 *Tom and Jerry Meet Mr. Fingers.* Carl Fallberg, reissue of 2006, four-color illustration, no cover price, 1973.

$2 $3 $4

5752 *Tom and Jerry Meet Mr. Fingers.* Identical to above, except a 39-cent cover price, 1974.

under $2.50 $3

5752-1 *Tom and Jerry Meet Mr. Fingers.* Identical to above, except black and white pix, 69-cent cover price and a different number, 1979.
under $.75 $1

5752-2 *Tom and Jerry Meet Mr. Fingers.* Identical to 5752-1, except a 79-cent cover price and a different number, 1980.
under $1

5765 *Tom and Jerry the Astro-Nots.* William Johnston, reissue of 2032, four-color illustration, no cover price, 1974.
$2 $3 $4

5765 *Tom and Jerry the Astro-Nots.* Identical to above, except a 39-cent cover price, 1974.
$1 $2 $3

5765 *Tom and Jerry the Astro-Nots.* Identical to above, except black and white pix and 49-cent cover price, 1975.
under $.75 $1

5765 *Tom and Jerry the Astro-Nots.* Identical to above, except a 69-cent cover price, 1977-1978.
under $.75 $1

5765-1 *Tom and Jerry the Astro-Nots.* Identical to above, except a different number, 1979.
under $1

5787-2 *Tom and Jerry Under the Big Top.* Jean Lewis, 79-cent cover price, 1980.
under $1 $1

5777 *Tweety and Sylvester, The Magic Voice.* Laura French and Rita Richie, 49-cent cover price, 1976.
under $1.25 $2

5777 *Tweety and Sylvester, The Magic Voice.* Identical to above, except a 69-cent cover price, 1977-1978.
under $.75 $1

5777-1 *Tweety and Sylvester, The Magic Voice.* Identical to above, except a different number, 1979.
under $1

5777-2 *Tweety and Sylvester, The Magic Voice.* Identical to 5777-1, except a 79-cent cover price and a different number, 1980.
under $1

5753 *Woody Woodpecker and the Meteor Menace.* Don R. Christensen, reissue of 2010, four-color illustration, no cover price, 1973.
$2 $3 $4

5753 *Woody Woodpecker and the Meteor Menace.* Identical to above, except a 39-cent cover price, 1974.
$1 $2 $3

5753-1 *Woody Woodpecker and the Meteor Menace.* Identical to above, except black and white pix, 69-cent cover price and a different number, 1979.
under $.75 $1

5753-2 *Woody Woodpecker and the Meteor Menace.* Identical to 5753-1, except a 79-cent cover price and a different number, 1980.
under $1

5763 *Woody Woodpecker, The Sinister Signal.* Vic Lockman, reissue of 2028, four-color illustration, no cover price, 1974.
$2 $3 $4

5763 *Woody Woodpecker, The Sinister Signal.* Identical to above, except a 39-cent cover price, 1974.
$1 $2 $3

5763 *Woody Woodpecker, The Sinister Signal.* Identical to above, except black and white pix and 69-cent cover price, 1977-1978.
under $1 $1

5763-1 *Woody Woodpecker, The Sinister Signal.* Identical to above, except a different number, 1979.
under $1 $1

Variant Big Little Books® (1933-1943)

With the conclusion of Whitman's lines of regular Big Little Books,® we come to the irregular, or variant, BLB formats. Briefly, these books are broken down into the following categories:
Big Big Books®
Big Little Nickel Books®
Famous Comics®
Famous Comics Cartoon Books® and Famous Funnies Cartoon Books®
Fast Action Stories® and Cartoon Story Books®
Nickel Books®
Penny Books®
Tall Comic Books®
Top-Line Comics®
Wee Little Books®
Miniatures
Giveaways

Miscellaneous (including a representative listing of BLB related books)
All of these books were published by Whitman (with the exception of the Fast Action Stories® and Cartoon Story Books,® which were made by Whitman for Dell Publishing Company).

Big Big Books® (1934-1938)

Big Big Books® are all 320 pages long and measure 7¼ x 9½ x 1¼ inches.

4069 *Buck Jones and the Night Riders.* Gaylord DuBois, Hal Arbo art, 1937.
　　　　　　　　$15　$30　$50

4057 *Buck Rogers on the Planetoid Eros, The Adventures of.* Phil Nowlan and Dick Calkins, 1934.
　　　　　　　　$30　$55　$90

4071 *Dick Tracy and the Mystery of the Purple Cross.* Chester Gould, scarce, 1938.
　　　　　　　　$30　$50　$70

4055 *Dick Tracy, Detective, The Adventures of.* Chester Gould, 1934.
　　　　　　　　$25　$40　$60

4055 *Dick Tracy, Detective, The Adventures of.* Chester Gould, as above, except a different cover, illustration on cover more refined (depicting Dick Tracy, Junior, and another scene), copyright 1934, but released in 1936.
　　　　　　　　$25　$40　$60

4054 *Little Orphan Annie, The Story of.* Harold Gray, 1934.
　　　　　　　　$25　$40　$60

4062 *Mickey Mouse and the Smugglers, The Story of.* Walt Disney Studios, 1935.
　　　　　　　　$30　$50　$70

4062 *Mickey Mouse and the Smugglers, The Story of.* Walt Disney Studios, as above, except a different cover, 1935.
$30 $50 $70

4063 *Popeye, Thimble Theatre Starring.* Elzie C. Segar, black spine, 1935.
$25 $40 $60

4063 *Popeye, Thimble Theatre Starring.* Elzie C. Segar, as above, except a different cover and a red spine, 1935.
$25 $40 $60

4056 *Skippy, The Story of.* Percy Crosby, 1934.
$15 $30 $50

4056 *Tarzan and the Tarzan Twins with Jad-Bal-Ja, the Golden Lion.* Edgar Rice Burroughs, 1936.
$30 $55 $85

4073 *Terry and the Pirates, The Adventures of.* Milton Caniff, 1938.
$20 $35 $53

4068 *Tom Mix and the Scourge of Paradise Valley.* Kathryn Heisenfelt, Henry Vallely art, 1937.
$20 $35 $53

Big Little Nickel Books® (1930s)

Big Little Nickel Books® were written for small children and contain 144 pages of stories in each book. Four titles were made in all, each measuring 3⅝ x 4⅜ x ¾ inches.

1005 *Blackie Bear and His Friends Book.*
$4 $7 $11

1006 *Blackie Bear Stories.*
$4 $7 $11

1007 *Folk Tales in Primer Style.*
$4 $8 $12

1008 *Folk Tales in Primer Style.*
$4 $8 $12

Famous Comics® (1934)

Famous Comics® came as a boxed set of three books, each containing three stories about popular comic strip characters. Each book is 96 pages long, soft-covered, and measures 3½ x 8½ x ¼ inches.

1 *The Katzenjammer Kids, Barney Google,* and *Little Jimmy,* 1934.
$7 $12 $16

2 *Polly and Her Pals, The Katzenjammer Kids,* and *Little Jimmy,* 1934.
$7 $12 $16

3 *Little Annie Rooney, The Katzenjammer Kids,* and *Polly and Her Pals,* 1934.
$7 $12 $16

684 All three books as a boxed set, 1934.
$25 $40 $55

Famous Comics Cartoon Books® and Famous Funnies Cartoon Books® (1934)

Famous Comics® and Famous Funnies Cartoon Books® were made in 1934. Both series had two titles each, for a total of four books. In format, these books are identical. They have 68 pages each, glued spines, and hard covers. They measure 7⅛ x 8 x ⅜ inches. Series 1201 has not yet been discovered.

1203 *Ella Cinders.* Charlie Plumb and Bill Conselman, Famous Funnies Cartoon Book,® 1934.
　　　　　　　　$8　$12　$20

1204 *Freckles and His Friends.* Merrill Blosser, Famous Comics Cartoon Book,® 1934.
　　　　　　　　$8　$12　$20

1200 *Captain and the Kids, The.* H.H. Knerr, Famous Funnies Cartoon Book,® 1934.
　　　　　　　　$8　$12　$20

1202 *Captain Easy and Wash Tubbs.* Roy Crane, Famous Comics Cartoon Book,® 1934.
　　　　　　　　$8　$12　$20

Fast Action Stories® and Cartoon Story Books® (1936, 1938-1943)

In 1936, Whitman produced four different hardcover titles, all numbered 6833. These books, called Cartoon Story Books,® sold for fifteen cents each. In addition to these, four soft-cover editions of the same books were also printed and sold for ten cents. These soft-cover versions are called Fast Action Stories® and are identical in size and content to the hardcover books. The soft-cover versions were marked "10¢," had a diamond-shaped Fast Action® logo, and were unnumbered. The series was discontinued in 1936, though other books were in preparation.

In 1938, Whitman picked up the Fast Action® books again and this time they continued until 1943. Although no hardcover Cartoon Story Books® were made during this period, some of these newer Fast Actions® still had the 6833 number. Most of the newer Fast Actions® went unnumbered, as actual numbers weren't assigned to the books until 1941. All of these books, the 1936 titles included, were made for Dell Publishing Company. However, because they employ popular Whitman BLB characters and were printed by Whitman, these books are included as Whitman variants. (See also Fawcett's Dime Action® books.) The 1936 books are listed first, then the books published in 1938-1943.

1936 Books

6833 *Dick Tracy, Detective and Federal Agent.* Chester Gould, Cartoon Story Book,® hc, 1936.
$15 $25 $40

nn *Dick Tracy, Detective and Federal Agent.* Chester Gould, Fast Action Story,® sc, 1936.
$11 $22 $33

6833 *Flash Gordon VS the Emperor of Mongo.* Alex Raymond, Cartoon Story Book,® hc, 1936.
$20 $30 $45

nn *Flash Gordon VS the Emperor of Mongo.* Alex Raymond, Fast Action Story,® sc, 1936.
$15 $25 $40

6833 *G-Man on Lightning Island.* Peter K. Maple, Henry E. Vallely art, Cartoon Story Book,® hc, 1936.
$10 $20 $28

nn *G-Man on Lightning Island.* Peter K. Maple, Henry E. Vallely art, Fast Action Story,® sc, 1936.
$9 $15 $22

1938-1943 Books

6833 *Tom Mix in the Riding Avenger.* Buck Wilson, Hal Arbo art, Cartoon Story Book,® hc, 1936.
$13 $24 $35

nn *Tom Mix in the Riding Avenger.* Buck Wilson, Hal Arbo art, Fast Action Story,® sc, 1936.
$10 $19 $27

15 *Andy Panda, The Adventures of.* Walter Lantz Productions, 1943.
$10 $19 $25

13 *Bugs Bunny and the Secret of Storm Island.* Leon Schlesinger Productions, 1942.
$10 $19 $25

nn *Charlie McCarthy and Edgar Bergen, The Adventures of.* Don Black, Henry E. Vallely art, 1938.
$10 $19 $25

nn *Dan Dunn, Secret Operative 48 and the Zeppelin of Doom.* Norman Marsh, 1938.
$13 $20 $28

nn *Dick Tracy and the Blackmailers.* Chester Gould, 1939.
$15 $25 $35

nn *Dick Tracy and the Chain of Evidence.* Chester Gould, 1938.
$19 $29 $39

9 *Dick Tracy and the Frozen Bullet Murders.* Chester Gould, 1941.
$14 $24 $32

nn *Dick Tracy and the Maroon Mask Gang.* Chester Gould, 1938.
$19 $29 $39

nn *Donald Duck and the Ducklings.* Walt Disney Studios, 1938.
$18 $27 $37

nn *Donald Duck, Out of Luck.* Walt Disney Studios, same cover as BLB 1434, different content, 1940.
$15 $25 $35

8 *Donald Duck Takes it on the Chin.* Walt Disney Studios, 1941.
$15 $25 $35

10 *Dumbo the Flying Elephant.* Walt Disney Studios, from BLB 1400, 1941.
$14 $24 $32

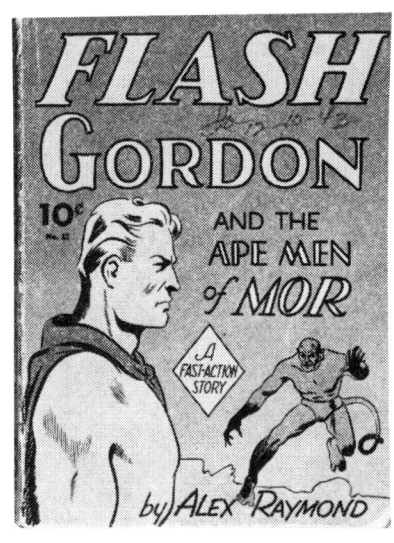

12 *Flash Gordon and the Ape Men of Mor.* Alex Raymond, 1942.
$23 $35 $47

nn *Gang Busters and Guns of Law.* Adapted from Phillips H. Lord's radio program, 1940.
$9 $17 $24

nn *Gene Autry in Gun Smoke.* Eleanor Packer, Henry E. Vallely art, 1938.
$10 $20 $30

nn *John Carter of Mars.* From Edgar Rice Burroughs, Alex Raymond art, from first comic strip, 1940.
$30 $45 $70

14 *Katzenjammer Kids, The.* H.H. Knerr, 1942.
$10 $20 $30

nn *King of the Royal Mounted, Policing the Frozen North.* Zane Grey, 1938.
$18 $27 $37

nn *Little Orphan Annie in Rags to Riches.* Harold Gray, 1938.
$18 $27 $37

nn *Little Orphan Annie Under the Big Top.* Harold Gray, 1938.
$18 $27 $37

nn *Lone Ranger and the Lost Valley, The.* Fran Striker, 1938.
$14 $24 $32

16 *Mickey Mouse and Pluto.* Floyd Gottfredson sty and art, 1942.
$20 $30 $40

nn *Mickey Mouse, The Sheriff of Nugget Gulch.* Floyd Gottfredson sty and art, 1938.
$23 $35 $47

nn *Mickey Mouse with Goofy and Mickey's Nephews.* Floyd Gottfredson sty and art, 1938.
$21 $33 $45

nn *Pinocchio and Jiminy Cricket.* Walt Disney Studios, art and sty content from BLB 1435, 1940.
$20 $30 $40

nn *Red Ryder Brings Law to Devil's Hole.* Fred Harman, 1939.
$13 $22 $31

11 *Smilin' Jack and the Border Bandits.* Zack Mosley, 1941.
$13 $22 $31

nn *Tailspin Tommy and the Airliner Mystery.* Hal Forrest, 1938.
$14 $24 $32

nn *Tailspin Tommy in Flying Aces.* Hal Forrest, 1938.
$14 $24 $32

nn *Tarzan the Avenger.* Edgar Rice Burroughs, 1939.
$20 $30 $40

nn *Tarzan with the Tarzan Twins in the Jungle.* Edgar Rice Burroughs, 1938.
$23 $35 $47

nn *Terry and the Pirates and the Mystery Ship.* Milton Caniff, 1938.
$15 $25 $35

nn *Tom Mix Avenges the Dry-Gulched Range King.* R.R. Winter (possibly a pseudonym for Russell R. Winterbotham), 1939.
$18 $27 $37

Nickel Books® (1937)

Nickel Books,® or the 1010 series, were printed with and without a 5-cent cover price and measure 5½ x 7½ x ¼ inches. They have cloth spines and an all-picture content. Also known as Famous Hardbound Cartoon Books,® there are four titles in this series.

1010 *Dan Dunn, Secret Operative 48 and the Gangsters' Frame-Up.* Norman Marsh, no 5-cent cover price, 1937.
$10 $15 $20

1010 *Dan Dunn, Secret Operative 48 and the Gangsters' Frame-Up.* As above, except a 5-cent cover price, 1937.
$8 $11 $15

1010 *King of the Royal Mounted in Arctic Law.* Zane Grey, no 5-cent cover price, 1937.
$11 $17 $23

1010 *King of the Royal Mounted in Arctic Law.* As above, except a 5-cent cover price, 1937.
$9 $14 $19

1010 *Little Orphan Annie and the Big Town Gunmen.* Harold Gray, no 5-cent cover price, 1937.
$11 $17 $23

1010 *Little Orphan Annie and the Big Town Gunmen.* As above, except a 5-cent cover price, 1937.
$9 $14 $19

1010 *Smokey Stover, Firefighter of Foo.* Bill Holman, no 5-cent cover price, 1937.
$10 $15 $20

1010 *Smokey Stover, Firefighter of Foo.* As above, except a 5-cent cover price, 1937.
$8 $11 $15

Penny Books® (1938-1939)

In one year, Whitman produced eighty-four titles as Penny Books.® They are very small, unnumbered BLBs with more text than pictures. Generally, those with printed advertisements on the back cover were given away by the store featured in the advertisement. Those with blank back covers were sold for a penny. There are five different numbered series of Penny Books,® and they are all presented here.

Famous Comic Strip Story Book Series® (1100A). Books in the 1100A series are 32 pages long and measure 2½ x 3½ x ⅛ inches. There are three variations of each title: (1) blue back covers, blank inside covers; (2) blue or orange back covers listing other titles in the series, blank inside covers; and (3) blue or orange back covers, inside front covers advertising the Better Little Books,® inside back covers promoting Dell comic books *Super Comics* and *Crackajack Funnies* (two comics that contained BLB characters). There is little, if any, preference among collectors as to which of these variations is most desirable. Consequently, all three variations are represented by a single listing.

Books without the added advertisement on the back covers are considered to be more desirable, and hence bring a slightly higher price. However, there are growing numbers who feel the advertisements for stores such as J.C. Penney's, add a bit of collectible nostalgia to the books. As a result, there is very little difference between the two values. As it stands, Penny Books® with blank back covers bring about 7 percent more on the market. Because this difference is negligible due to the inherently lower value of Penny Books,® the prices listed here are for those books without the added advertisement.

nn *Alley Oop and the Missing King of Moo.* Vince T. Hamlin, 1938.
$5 $10 $15

nn *Dan Dunn, Secret Operative 48 and the Bank Hold-Up.* Norman Marsh, 1938.
$4 $8 $12

nn *Dan Dunn, Secret Operative 48 Plays a Lone Hand.* Norman Marsh, 1938.
$4 $8 $12

nn *Dick Tracy Gets His Man.* Chester Gould, 1938.
$6 $12 $18

nn *Dick Tracy the Detective.* Chester Gould, 1938.
$6 $12 $18

nn *Don Winslow of the U.S. Navy and the Missing Admiral.* Frank V. Martinek, 1938.
$4 $8 $12

nn *Freckles and His Friends Stage a Play.* Merrill Blosser, 1938.
$3 $6 $9

nn *G-Men and the Missing Clues.* K.H. Eisen, 1938.
$3 $5 $8

nn *G-Men on the Job Again.* K.H. Eisen, 1938.
$3 $5 $8

nn *Ken Maynard in Six-Gun Law.* Eleanor Packer, 1938.
$3 $5 $8

nn *Little Orphan Annie Gets into Trouble.* Harold Gray, 1938.
$6 $12 $18

nn *Little Orphan Annie Saves Sandy.* Harold Gray, 1938.
$6 $12 $18

nn *Smilin' Jack, Grounded on a Tropical Shore.* Zack Mosley, 1938.
$4 $8 $12

nn *Smokey Stover and the Fire Chief of Foo.* Bill Holman, 1938.
$4 $8 $12

nn *Terry and the Pirates, The Adventures of.* Milton Caniff, 1938.
$5 $10 $15

nn *Terry and the Pirates on Their Travels.* Milton Caniff, 1938.
$5 $10 $15

nn *Texas Ranger in the West, The.* Albert Shore, 1938.
$2 $4 $6

nn *Texas Ranger to the Rescue, The.* Albert Shore, 1938.
$2 $4 $6

Fun Book Series® (1100B). The 1100B series Penny Books® are like the 1100A series books, except for content and the fact that there are no variations of each title. Prices are for books without ads.

nn *Dreams.* 1938.
$2 $4 $6

nn *Fortune Teller.* 1938.
$2 $4 $6

nn *Fun, Puzzles, and Riddles.* 1938.
$2 $4 $6

nn *Hobbies.* 1938.
$2 $4 $6

nn *Jokes, Laughs Galore.* 1938.
$2 $4 $6

nn *Jokes, Side Splitting.* 1938.
$2 $4 $6

nn *Learn to be a Ventriloquist.* 1938.
$2 $4 $6

nn *Magic, How to Do Tricks.* 1938.
$2 $4 $6

nn *Magic Tricks Explained.* 1938.
$2 $4 $6

nn *Movie Jokes.* 1938.
$2 $4 $6

nn *Puzzle Book.* 1938.
$2 $4 $6

nn *Puzzles.* 1938.
$2 $4 $6

nn *Quiz Book.* 1938.
$2 $4 $6

nn *Riddles for Fun.* 1938.
$2 $4 $6

nn *Riddles to Guess.* 1938.
$2 $4 $6

nn *Tell Your Fortune.* 1938.
$2 $4 $6

nn *Tricks Easy to Do.* 1938.
$2 $4 $6

nn *Tricks You Can Do.* 1938.
$2 $4 $6

Cowboy and Detective Story Book Series® (1101). The 1101 series Penny Books® are identical to the 1100A and 1100B series books in format. Story lines are based on BLB characters, for the most part. There are two variations of the 1101 books without store advertisements: (1) orange back covers, blank inside covers; and (2) orange back covers, inside front covers advertising titles in the Better Little Book® series, inside back covers promoting Dell comic books *Super Comics* and *Crackajack Funnies*. Prices are for either variation, minus advertisements.

nn *Buck Jones on the Six-Gun Trail.* Don Black, Harry Lawson art, 1939.
$4 $8 $12

nn *Fighting Cowboy of Nugget Gulch, The.* 1939.
$2 $4 $6

nn *Gang Busters and the Radio Clues.* Isaac McAnally, 1939.
$4 $8 $12

nn *George O'Brien and the Arizona Badman.* Eleanor Packer, 1939.
$4 $8 $12

nn *Ghost Gun Gang Meet Their Match, The.* 1939.
$3 $6 $9

nn *Jack King of the Secret Service and the Counterfeiters.* John Gray, 1939.
$3 $6 $9

nn *Jim Brant of the Highway Patrol and the Mysterious Accident.* 1939.
$2 $4 $6

nn *Jim Doyle Private Detective and the Train Hold-Up.* Ernest New, 1939.
$2 $4 $6

nn *Junior G-Men Solve a Crime.* Morrell Massey (?), 1939.
$3 $6 $9

nn *King of the Royal Mounted in Law of the North.* From Zane Grey, 1939.
$5 $10 $15

nn *Lightning Jim Whipple, U.S. Marshall in Indian Territory.* Based on the radio show, 1939.
$3 $6 $9

nn *Red Ryder and the Highway Robbers.* Fred Harman, 1939.
$4 $8 $12

nn *Sandy Gregg, Federal Agent on Special Assignment.* 1939.
$3 $5 $8

nn *Tom Beatty, Ace Detective and the Gorgon Gang.* Rex Loomis (?), 1939.
$4 $8 $12

nn *Tom Beatty, Ace of the Service and the Kidnappers.* Rex Loomis (?), 1939.
$4 $8 $12

nn *Tom Mix Rides to the Rescue.* 1939.
$5 $10 $15

nn *Two-Gun Montana Shoots it Out.* Tex Reynolds, 1939.
$4 $8 $12

Fairy Tales® and Story Book Series® (1104). The 1104 series Penny Books® are more square than books in the preceding series and measure 2¾ x 3 x ⅛ inches. They are 32 pages long and have a cloth binding wrapped around the stapled spine, rather than just a black printed edge like the other Penny Books®. Prices are for books without ads.

nn *Beauty and the Beast.* 1939.
$3 $5 $8

nn *Chicken Greedy.* 1939.
$3 $5 $8

nn *Chicken Licken.* 1939.
$3 $5 $8

nn *Dick Whittington and His Cat.* 1939.
$3 $5 $8

nn *East of the Sun and West of the Moon.* 1939.
$3 $5 $8

nn *Gingerbread Boy, The.* 1939.
$3 $5 $8

nn *Hansel and Grethel.* 1939.
$3 $5 $8

nn *Little Black Sambo.* 1939.
$4 $8 $12

nn *Little Polly Flinders.* 1939.
$3 $5 $8

nn *Little Red Hen, The.* 1939.
$3 $5 $8

nn *Little Red Riding Hood.* 1939.
$3 $5 $8

nn *Musicians of Bremen, The.* 1939.
$3 $5 $8

nn *Patch.* 1939.
$3 $5 $8

nn *Peter Rabbit.* 1939.
$3 $5 $8

nn *Puss-in-Boots.* 1939.
$3 $5 $8

nn *Red Hen and the Fox, The.* 1939.
$3 $5 $8

nn *Three Bears, The.* 1939.
$3 $5 $8

nn *Three Little Pigs, The.* 1939.
$3 $5 $8

nn *Tim the Builder.* 1939.
$3 $5 $8

nn *Ugly Duckling, The.* 1939.
$3 $5 $8

Walt Disney Picture Story Book Series® (1145). The 1145 series Penny Books® are 12 pages long, measure 4¼ x 4¾ x ⅛ inches, and contain full four-color illustrations. They are based on Walt Disney cartoons of the same name and are very scarce, especially in better condition. There were ten titles made. None had advertisements.

nn	*Brave Little Tailor, The.* 1939.	$7	$12	$18
nn	*Donald Duck's Cousin Gus.* 1939.	$7	$12	$18
nn	*Donald's Better Self.* 1939.	$7	$12	$18
nn	*Donald's Lucky Day.* 1939.	$8	$13	$20
nn	*Farmyard Symphony.* 1939.	$7	$12	$18
nn	*Goofy and Wilbur.* 1939.	$7	$12	$18
nn	*Mickey's Gold Rush.* 1939.	$8	$13	$20
nn	*Pluto at the Society Dog Show.* 1939.	$7	$12	$18
nn	*Practical Pig, The.* 1939.	$6	$11	$15
nn	*Ugly Duckling, The.* 1939.	$7	$12	$18

Tall Comic Books® (early 1940s)

Tall Comic Books® are actually variations of the all-picture Big Little Books.® Three Tall Comic Books® emerged in the 1940s, each 200 pages long and measuring 3¾ x 8¼ x ¼ inches. Whitman took the story lines from daily comic strips and comic books.

531 *Andy Panda.* Walter Lantz Productions, Tall Comic Book,® all-pix, 1943.
$8 $15 $20

530 *Bugs Bunny.* Leon Schlesinger Productions, Tall Comic Book,® all-pix, reprints comic Looney Tunes 1, scarce, 1943.
$15 $22 $33

532 *Mickey's Dog Pluto.* Walt Disney Studios, Tall Comic Book,® all-pix, 1943.
$12 $20 $30

Top-Line Comics® (1935)

In 1935, Whitman put out four numbered, boxed sets of Top-Line Comics.® Each set contains three unnumbered titles in BLB format. These books are soft-covered, 160 pages long, and measure 3½ x 2½ inches.

nn *Bobby Thatcher and the Samarang Emerald.* George Storm, from set 540, 1935.
$7 $12 $18

nn *Broncho Bill in Suicide Canyon.* Harry F. O'Neill, from set 540, 1935.
$7 $12 $18

nn *Freckles and His Friends in the North Woods.* Merrill Blosser, from set 540, 1935.
$7 $12 $18

540 All three books above as a boxed set, 1935.
$30 $45 $60

nn *Little Joe and the City of Gangsters.* Ed Leffingwell, from set 541, 1935.
$6 $10 $15

nn *Smilin' Jack and His Flivver Plane.* Zack Mosley, from set 541, 1935.
$8 $14 $21

nn *Streaky and the Football Signals.* Gus Edson, from set 541, 1935.
$7 $12 $18

541 All three books above as a boxed set, 1935.
$30 $45 $60

nn *Dinglehoofer und His Dog Adolph.* H.H. Knerr, from set 542, 1935.
$7 $12 $18

nn *Jungle Jim.* Alex Raymond, from set 542, 1935.
$10 $16 $25

nn *Sappo.* E.C. Segar, from set 542, 1935.
$9 $15 $23

542 All three books above as a boxed set, 1935.
$35 $52 $72

nn *Alexander Smart, Esq.* Doc Winner, from set 543, 1935.
$6 $10 $15

nn *Bunky.* Billy DeBeck, from set 543, 1935.
$6 $10 $15

nn *Nicodemus O'Malley.* Ad Carter, from set 543, 1935.
$6 $10 $15

543 All three books above as a boxed set, 1935.
$27 $39 $51

Wee Little Books® (1934)

Prior to putting out the Top-Line Comic® boxed sets, Whitman published six sets of six books called Wee Little Books.® The sets came in numbered boxes, with each book measuring 3¼ x 3⅝ inches and having forty pages. The Little Orphan Annie set is unnumbered, and was given away through the Little Orphan Annie Shake-up Mug contest. Contest entrants received the first title and instructions to send in one aluminum seal from Ovaltine cans for each of the other titles in the set. Subscribers to the *Mickey Mouse Magazine* received the Mickey Mouse Wee Little Book® set free.

512 All six books listed below as a boxed set, Floyd Gottfredson sty and art, 1934.
$40 $70 $100

nn   *Mickey Mouse and Tanglefoot.* 1934.
$6 $9 $12

nn   *Mickey Mouse at the Carnival.* 1934.
$6 $9 $12

nn   *Mickey Mouse Will Not Quit.* 1934.
$6 $9 $12

nn   *Mickey Mouse Wins the Race.* 1934.
$6 $9 $12

nn   *Mickey Mouse's Misfortune.* 1934.
$6 $9 $12

nn   *Mickey Mouse's Up Hill Fight.* 1934.
$6 $9 $12

513 All six books listed below as a boxed set, from children's classics, 1934.
$25 $40 $53

nn   *Child's Garden of Verses.* 1934.
$3 $5 $8

nn   *Happy Prince, The.* 1934.
$3 $5 $8

nn   *Joan of Arc.* 1934.
$3 $5 $8

nn   *Peter Pan.* 1934.
$3 $5 $8

nn   *Pied Piper of Hamlin.* 1934.
$3 $5 $8

nn   *Robin Hood.* 1934.
$3 $5 $8

514 All six books listed below as a boxed set, from *Mother Goose,* art by Mary Royt, 1934.
$20 $32 $48

nn   *Jack and Jill.* 1934.
$2 $4 $7

nn   *Little Bo Peep.* 1934.
$2 $4 $7

nn   *Little Tommy Tucker.* 1934.
$2 $4 $7

nn   *Mother Goose.* 1934.
$2 $4 $7

nn   *Old King Cole.* 1934.
$2 $4 $7

nn   *Simple Simon.* 1934.
$2 $4 $7

518 All six books listed below as a boxed set, from the *Burgess Stories*, written and illustrated by Thornton Burgess, 1934.
$20 $32 $48

nn *Betty Bear's Lesson*. 1934.
$2 $4 $7

nn *Jimmy Skunk's Justice*. 1934.
$2 $4 $7

nn *Little Joe Otter's Slide*. 1934.
$2 $4 $7

nn *Peter Rabbit's Carrots*. 1934.
$2 $4 $7

nn *Unc' Billy Gets Even*. 1934.
$2 $4 $7

nn *Whitefoot's Secret*. 1934.
$2 $4 $7

519 All six books listed below as a boxed set, from *Bible Stories*, art by Helen Janes, 1934.
$25 $40 $53

nn *Daniel, The Story of*. 1934.
$3 $5 $8

nn *David, The Story of*. 1934.
$3 $5 $8

nn *Gideon, The Story of*. 1934.
$3 $5 $8

nn *Joseph, The Story of*. 1934.
$3 $5 $8

nn *Moses, The Story of*. 1934.
$3 $5 $8

nn *Ruth and Naomi, The Story of*. 1934.
$3 $5 $8

nn All six books listed below as a boxed set, Harold Gray sty and art, 1934.
$35 $58 $90

nn *Little Orphan Annie and Daddy Warbucks*. 1934.
$5 $8 $11

nn *Little Orphan Annie and Her Dog Sandy*. 1934.
$5 $8 $11

nn *Little Orphan Annie and the Lucky Knife*. 1934.
$5 $8 $11

nn *Little Orphan Annie and the Pinch-Pennys*. 1934.
$5 $8 $11

nn *Little Orphan Annie at Happy Home*. 1934.
$5 $8 $11

nn *Little Orphan Annie Finds Mickey*. 1934.
$5 $8 $11

Miniatures (1930s)

A rare category of Big Little Books® is the Whitman miniatures. Only a handful are known to exist. Each is a shortened version of a regular BLB that, curiously, has the different three-color soft-cover variation that occurred in the early 700 and 1100 series, all in 1934 and 1935. From this pattern, we can assume that other BLBs with a different three-color soft-cover variation could possibly have miniature counterparts as well. No one knows what the miniatures' intended market was. Were they giveaways? They most likely emerged as a result of experiments Whitman conducted to test various BLB formats. If other miniatures do exist, they are certain to excite the collector's imagination. All have soft, three-color covers.

nn *Captain Easy, Soldier of Fortune.* Roy Crane, 48 pages, 3½ x 5⅝ inches, adapted from 1125, very rare, 1935.
$15 $30 $50

nn *Dick Tracy Solves the Penfield Mystery.* Chester Gould, 48 pages, 3½ x 5⅝ inches, adapted from 1137, very rare, 1935.
$25 $47 $80

nn *Don Winslow, U.S.N.* Frank V. Martinek, I.A. Beroth art, 48 pages, 3½ x 5⅝ inches, adapted from 1107, very rare, 1935.
$18 $35 $55

nn *Eric Noble and the Forty-Niners.* Lloyd E. Smith, B. McNaughton art, 48 pages, 3½ x 5⅝ inches, adapted from 772, very rare, 1935.
$15 $25 $40

nn *Flash Gordon and the Monsters of Mongo.* Alex Raymond, 48 pages, 3½ x 5⅝ inches, adapted from 1166, very rare, 1935.
$40 $60 $100

nn *Little Orphan Annie and the Ghost Gang.* Harold Gray, 48 pages, 3½ x 5⅝ inches, adapted from 1154, very rare, 1935.
$25 $47 $80

nn *Mickey Mouse and the Bat Bandit.* Floyd Gottfredson, 48 pages, 3½ x 5⅝ inches, adapted from 1153, very rare, 1935.
$30 $50 $90

nn *Moon Mullins and the Plushbottom Twins.* Frank Willard, 48 pages, 3½ x 5⅝ inches, adapted from 1134, very rare, 1935.
$18 $35 $55

nn *Prairie Bill and the Covered Wagon.* G.A. Alkire, 48 pages, 3½ x 5⅝ inches, adapted from 758, very rare, 1935.
$15 $25 $40

nn *Tarzan Twins, The.* Edgar Rice Burroughs, 48 pages, 3½ x 5⅝ inches, adapted from 770, very rare, 1935.
$30 $50 $90

nn *Tom Mix in the Fighting Cowboy.* Leon Morgan, 48 pages, 3½ x 5⅝ inches, adapted from 1144, very rare, 1935.
$20 $40 $60

Giveaways (1933-1938)

If the miniature Big Little Books® are the rarest, the giveaways are easily the most diverse. Whitman produced many different titles for various companies to be given away as promotional items. The giveaways are divided into five groups: (1) traditional (the Cocomalts and other giveaways that most resemble regular BLBs); (2) rectangular (the long, thin giveaways distributed by the Karmetz and Perkins agencies for such companies as Sears, Kool-Aid, and Pan-Am Gas); (3) Pan-Am (those giveaways made solely for Pan-Am Gas, not to be confused with the rectangular giveaways bearing Pan-Am ads); (4) Ice-Cream (the Tarzan Cup-Lid® and Buddy Book® ice-cream premiums); and (5) miscellaneous (the various one-shot and unusual giveaways). The second and third categories contain books with and without advertising. Those without ads are considered rare and are worth considerably more than those with advertising. For additional description, see the section in the introduction entitled "Giveaways, Miniatures, and Other Variants."

Traditional Giveaways

nn *Alley Oop in the Invasion of Moo.* V.T. Hamlin, Cocomalt, 256 pages, 1935.
$15 $25 $35

nn *Billy the Kid, Western Outlaw, The.* Hal Arbo art, from BLB 773, Cocomalt, 256 pages, 1935.
$10 $18 $25

nn *Buck Rogers in the City of Floating Globes.* Phil Nowlan and Dick Calkins, Cocomalt, 200 pages, 1935.
$20 $35 $50

nn *Buck Rogers in the 25th Century A.D.* Phil Nowlan and Dick Calkins, from BLB 742, Cocomalt, 200 pages, 1933.
$15 $25 $35

nn *Buck Rogers on the Moons of Saturn.* Phil Nowlan and Dick Calkins, from BLB 1143, Cocomalt, very scarce, 200 pages, 1934.
$20 $38 $55

nn *Buffalo Bill, The Wild West Adventures of.* Hal Arbo art, Cocomalt, 200 pages, 1935.
$10 $18 $25

nn *Captain Easy and Wash Tubbs.* Roy Crane, from BLB 751 *(Wash Tubbs in Pandemonia)*, Cocomalt, 256 pages, 1934.
$13 $20 $28

nn *Chester Gump at Silver Creek Ranch.* Sidney Smith, from BLB 766, 200 pages, 1933.
$13 $20 $28

nn *Houdini's Big Little Book of Magic.* Harry Houdini, from BLB 715, Cocomalt, 200 pages, dated 1927 but actually 1933.
$10 $18 $25

nn *Houdini's Big Little Book of Magic.* As above, except Amoco (American Gas) ad, larger size, eight fewer pages, dated 1927 but actually 1933.
$15 $25 $35

nn *King of the Royal Mounted.* Zane Grey, from BLB 1103, Cocomalt, 256 pages, 1935.
    $15 $25 $35

nn *Men of the Mounted.* Ted McCall, from BLB 755, Cocomalt, 200 pages, 1934.
    $10 $18 $25

nn *Mickey Mouse Sails for Treasure Island.* Floyd Gottfredson, from BLB 750, no ad, 192 pages, scarce, 1933.
    $15 $25 $35

nn *Mickey Mouse Sails for Treasure Island.* As above, except a Kolynos Dental Cream radio giveaway, 1933.
    $15 $25 $35

nn *Mickey Mouse, The Mail Pilot.* Floyd Gottfredson, large size, Amoco (American Gas) ad, from BLB 731, 288 pages, 1933.
    $10 $18 $25

nn *Moon Mullins and Kayo.* Frank Willard, from BLB 746, Cocomalt, 200 pages, 1933.
    $10 $18 $25

nn *Reg'lar Fellers.* Gene Byrnes, from BLB 754, Cocomalt, 200 pages, 1933.
    $10 $18 $25

nn *Skippy, The Story of.* Percy Crosby, from BLB 761, Phillips Dental Magnesia ad, 200 pages, 1934.
    $15 $25 $35

nn *Smitty, Golden Gloves Tournament.* Walter Berndt, from BLB 745, Cocomalt, 200 pages, 1934.
    $13 $20 $28

nn *Tailspin Tommy in Wings Over the Arctic.* Hal Forrest, from BLB 1124 (*Tailspin Tommy, The Dirigible Flight to the North Pole*), Cocomalt, 200 pages, 1934.
    $15 $25 $35

nn *Texas Ranger, The.* Leon Morgan, Hal Arbo art, from BLB 1135, Cocomalt, 256 pages, 1936.
    $10 $18 $25

Rectangular Giveaways

nn *Chester Gump at the Silver Creek Ranch.* Sidney Smith, from BLB 734, 48 pages, 4⅛ x 5⅝ inches, Karmetz, no ad, 1933.
    $10 $18 $25

nn *Chester Gump at the Silver Creek Ranch.* As above, except added advertisement, 1933.
    $8 $13 $18

nn *Chester Gump Finds the Hidden Treasure.* Sidney Smith, from BLB 766, 48 pages, 4⅛ x 5⅝ inches, Karmetz, wide blank margins, no ad, 1934.
    $10 $18 $25

nn *Chester Gump Finds the Hidden Treasure.* As above, except added advertisement, 1934.
    $8 $13 $18

nn *Chester Gump Finds the Hidden Treasure.* Sidney Smith, from BLB 766, 48 pages, 3½ x 5¾, Perkins, no wide blank cover margins, no ad, 1934.
$10 $18 $25

nn *Chester Gump Finds the Hidden Treasure.* As above, except added advertisement, 1934.
$8 $13 $18

nn *Cowboy Stories.* Leon Morgan, Hal Arbo art, from BLB 724, 48 pages, 4⅛ x 5⅝ inches, Karmetz, no ad, 1933.
$10 $18 $25

nn *Cowboy Stories.* As above, except added advertisement, 1933.
$8 $13 $18

nn *Dick Tracy and Dick Tracy, Jr.* Chester Gould, from BLB 710, 48 pages, 4⅛ x 5⅝ inches, Karmetz, no ad, 1933.
$15 $25 $35

nn *Dick Tracy and Dick Tracy, Jr.* As above, except added advertisement, 1933.
$13 $20 $29

nn *Dick Tracy, The Adventures of.* Chester Gould, from BLB 707, 48 pages, 4⅛ x 5⅝ inches, Karmetz, no ad, 1933.
$15 $30 $45

nn *Dick Tracy, The Adventures of.* As above, except added advertisement, 1933.
$13 $23 $33

nn *Dick Tracy the Detective and Dick Tracy, Jr.* Chester Gould, from BLB 710, 48 pages, 3½ x 5¾ inches, Perkins, no ad, 1933.
$15 $25 $35

nn *Dick Tracy the Detective and Dick Tracy, Jr.* As above, except added advertisement, 1933.
$13 $20 $29

nn *Ella Cinders and the Mysterious House.* Charlie Plumb and Bill Conselman, from BLB 1106, 48 pages, 3½ x 5¾ inches, Perkins, no ad, 1934.
$10 $18 $25

nn *Ella Cinders and the Mysterious House.* As above, except added advertisement, 1934.
$8 $13 $18

nn *Little Orphan Annie.* Harold Gray, from BLB 708, 48 pages, 4⅛ x 5⅝ inches, Karmetz, no ad, dated 1928 but actually 1933.
$15 $30 $45

nn *Little Orphan Annie.* As above, except added advertisement, 1933.
$13 $23 $33

nn *Little Orphan Annie and Sandy.* Harold Gray, from BLB 716, 48 pages, 4⅛ x 5⅝ inches, Karmetz, no ad. 1933.
$15 $25 $35

nn *Little Orphan Annie and Sandy.* As above, except added advertisement, 1933.
$13 $20 $29

nn *Men of the Mounted.* Ted McCall, from BLB 755, 48 pages, 3½ x 5¾ inches, Perkins, no ad, 1934.
$10 $18 $25

nn *Men of the Mounted.* As above, except added advertisement, 1934.
$8 $13 $18

nn *Tailspin Tommy, The Pay-Roll Mystery.* Hal Forrest, from BLB 747, 48 pages, 3½ x 5¾ inches, Perkins, no ad, 1934.
$15 $25 $35

nn *Tailspin Tommy, The Pay-Roll Mystery.* As above, except added advertisement, 1934.
$13 $20 $29

nn *Tarzan of the Apes.* Edgar Rice Burroughs, redrawn from Hal Foster strip, from BLB 744, 48 pages, 3½ x 5¾ inches, Perkins, no ad, 1933.
$15 $30 $40

nn *Tarzan of the Apes.* As above, except added advertisement, 1933.
$13 $23 $30

nn *Tarzan Twins, The.* Edgar Rice Burroughs, from BLB 770, 48 pages, 3½ x 5¾ inches, Perkins, no ad, 1935.
$15 $30 $40

nn *Tarzan Twins, The.* As above, except added advertisement, 1935.
$13 $23 $30

nn *Terry and the Pirates.* Milton Caniff, from BLB 1156, 48 pages, 3½ x 5¾ inches, Perkins, no ad, 1935.
$13 $23 $30

nn *Terry and the Pirates.* As above, except added advertisement, 1935.
$10 $18 $25

nn *Wash Tubbs.* Roy Crane, from BLB 751, 48 pages, 4⅛ x 5⅝ inches, Karmetz, no ad, 1934.
$10 $18 $25

nn *Wash Tubbs.* As above, except added advertisement, 1934.
$8 $13 $18

Pan-Am Giveaways

nn *Dan Dunn Meets Chang Loo.* Norman Marsh, 64 pages, 3½ x 3¼ inches, no known distributor, no ad, 1938.
$15 $25 $35

nn *Dan Dunn Meets Chang Loo.* As above, except Pan-Am Gas ad, 1938.
$13 $23 $30

nn *G-Men in Kidnap Justice.* 64 pages, 3½ x 3¼ inches, no known distributor, no ad, 1938.
$10 $18 $25

nn *G-Men in Kidnap Justice.* As above, except Pan-Am Gas ad, 1938.
$8 $13 $18

nn *Little Orphan Annie in Hollywood.* Harold Gray, 64 pages, 3½ x 3¼ inches, no known distributor, no ad, 1937.
$15 $30 $45

nn *Little Orphan Annie in Hollywood.* As above, except Pan-Am Gas ad, 1937.
$13 $23 $33

nn *Tarzan and the Daring Rescue.* Edgar Rice Burroughs, 64 pages, 3½ x 3¼ inches, no known distributor, 1938.
$15 $30 $45

nn *Tarzan and the Daring Rescue.* As above, except Pan-Am Gas ad, 1938.
$13 $23 $33

nn *Tarzan and the Golden City.* Edgar Rice Burroughs, 64 pages, 3½ x 3¼ inches, no known distributor, 1938.
$15 $30 $45

nn *Tarzan and the Golden City.* As above, except Pan-Am Gas ad, 1938.
$13 $23 $33

Ice-Cream Giveaways

These premiums are divided into two subgroups: the Tarzan Ice-Cream Cup-Lid® giveaways (1934-1936) and the Buddy Book Ice-Cream® giveaways (1938).

Tarzan Ice-Cream Giveaways. A listing for the Tarzan Ice-Cream Cup-Lid® giveaways follows:

nn *Broncho Bill*. Harry F. O'Neill, 3¾ x 4⅛ inches, 144 pages, 1935.
$12 $20 $30

nn *Buck Rogers*. Phil Nowlan and Dick Calkins, 3¾ x 4⅛ inches, 144 pages, 1935.
$18 $28 $45

5 *Chester Gump and His Friends*. Sidney Smith, 3¾ x 3⅝ inches, 128 pages, 1934.
$12 $20 $30

nn *Cowboys of the West*. Zane Grey, 3¾ x 4⅛ inches, 144 pages, 1935.
$12 $20 $30

9 *Dan Dunn's Mysterious Ride*. Norman Marsh, 3¾ x 3⅝ inches, 128 pages, 1934.
$14 $24 $35

3 *Dick Tracy Meets a New Gang*. Chester Gould, 3¾ x 3⅝ inches, 128 pages, 1934.
$15 $25 $40

nn *Ella Cinders*. Charlie Plumb and Bill Conselman, 3¾ x 4⅛ inches, 144 pages, 1935.
$12 $20 $30

11 *Ella Cinders' Exciting Experience*. Charlie Plumb and Bill Conselman, 3¾ x 3⅝ inches, 128 pages, 1934.
$12 $20 $30

4 *G-Men Foil the Kidnappers*. Cliff Junceau, 3¾ x 3⅝ inches, 128 pages, 1936.
$12 $20 $30

8 *Little Mary Mixup Wins a Prize*. R.M. Brinkerhoff, 3¾ x 3⅝ inches, 128 pages, 1936.
$12 $20 $30

2 *Smitty and Herby*. Walter Berndt, 3¾ x 3⅝ inches, 128 pages, 1934.
$12 $20 $30

nn *Tailspin Tommy*. Hal Forrest, 3¾ x 4⅛ inches, 144 pages, 1935.
$14 $24 $35

7 *Tailspin Tommy's Perilous Adventure*. Hal Forrest, 3¾ x 3⅝ inches, 128 pages, 1934.
$14 $24 $35

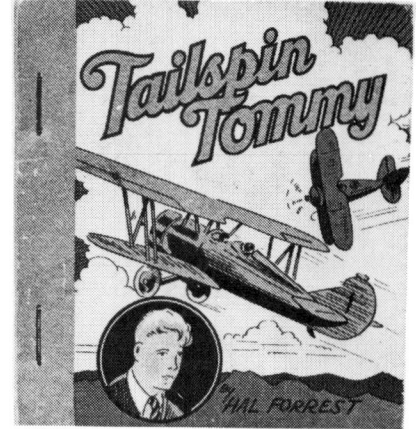

nn *Tarzan.* Edgar Rice Burroughs, 3¾ x 4⅛ inches, 144 pages, 1935.
$15 $25 $40

1 *Tarzan and His Jungle Friends.* Edgar Rice Burroughs, 3¾ x 3⅝ inches, 128 pages, 1934.
$15 $25 $40

10 *Terry and the Pirates Meet Again.* Milton Caniff, 3¾ x 3⅝ inches, 128 pages, 1936.
$14 $24 $35

12 *Texas Ranger, Rustler Strategy, The.* Cliff Junceau, 3¾ x 3⅝ inches, 128 pages, 1936.
$12 $20 $30

6 *Wash Tubbs' Foreign Travels.* Roy Crane, 3¾ x 3⅝ inches, 128 pages, 1934.
$12 $20 $30

Buddy Book Ice-Cream Giveaways. All books measure 3½ x 3½ inches and are 126 pages long.

8 *Buck Jones in Cowboy Masquerade.* Don Black, 1938.
$12 $20 $30

6 *Dan Dunn, Secret Operative 48 and the Counterfeiter Ring.* Norman Marsh, 1938.
$14 $24 $35

11 *Dick Tracy in Smashing the Famon Racket.* Chester Gould, 1938.
$15 $25 $40

12 *G-Man VS the Underworld Chief.* W.W. Engleton, 1938.
$12 $20 $30

7 *Kayo and Moon Mullins Way Down South.* Frank Willard, 1938.
$14 $24 $35

5 *King of the Royal Mounted in the Far North.* Zane Grey, 1938.
$14 $24 $35

2 *Smilin' Jack and His Stratosphere Plane.* Zack Mosley, 1938.
$14 $24 $35

1 *Smokey Stover, The Fireman of Foo.* Bill Holman, 1938.
$12 $20 $30

3 *Tailspin Tommy on the Mountain of Human Sacrifice.* Hal Forrest, 1938.
$15 $25 $40

4 *Terry and the Pirates Ashore in Singapore.* Milton Caniff, 1938.
$14 $24 $35

10 *Tim McCoy Fighting the Redskins.* Buck Wilson, Robert Weisman art, this book and the following one have the same number (one should be 9), 1938.
$14 $24 $35

10 *Tom Mix in the Tepee Ranch Mystery.* This book and the preceding one have the same number (one should be 9), 1938.
$15 $25 $40

Miscellaneous Giveaways

This group is made up of various premiums that can't be included with the other major categories. Possibly, some of these titles were not made by Whitman. They are included here because they either feature Whitman BLB characters, or are similar to other Whitman books. Those definitely made by Whitman are designated as such.

nn *Dick Tracy's Secret Detective Methods and Magic Tricks.* Chester Gould, 5 x 7½ inches, 64 pages, sc, Quaker Oats premium, 1939.
$15 $25 $40

nn *Flash Brown the Super Scientist.* Small gum or penny book premium, color illustration, several different volumes possible, price is per book, 1930s.
$7 $12 $17

nn *Gumps in Radioland, The.* Gus Edson, 3¾ x 5½ inches, 96 pages, Pebeco Toothpaste premium, similar to FA (Fast Action), sc, scarce, 1937.
$20 $30 $40

nn *Mickey Mouse and Minnie at Macy's.* Walt Disney Studios, Whitman, 3⅓ x 3⅔ inches, 144 pages, sc, made for Macy's Department Store, rare, 1934.
$35 $55 $75

nn *Mickey Mouse and Minnie March to Macy's.* Walt Disney Studios, Whitman, 3⅓ x 3⅔ inches, 144 pages, sc, made for Macy's Department Store, rare, 1935.
$35 $55 $75

nn *Mickey Mouse and the Magic Carpet.* Walt Disney Studios, Whitman, 3½ x 4 inches, 144 pages, sc, made for Kay Kamen Department Store, rare, 1935.
$30 $45 $60

1-24 *Tom Mix National Chicle Gum Premiums.* Sponsored by the National Chicle Gum Company (possibly the originators of the Flash Brown title as well), these were eight-page booklets with two-color soft covers and BLB format interior. At the time of this printing, twenty-four titles are known to exist, with others possible. Price is per book, scarce, 1934.
$8 $15 $22

nn *Tom Mix, The Trail of the Terrible Six.* Tom Mix, sponsored by the Ralston Purina Company, 3 x 3½ inches, 80 pages, 1937.
$8 $15 $22

Miscellaneous BLBs and Related Books (1930s-1940s)

The following section includes representative listings of many types of books that collectors include with Big Little Books.® While some of these entries may not be from the Whitman line (most notably the Blue Ribbon pop-ups), they are listed here because of their similarity to other Whitman books, or because they contain Whitman BLB characters. Most, however, are Whitman products and are frequently sought by serious collectors of Big Little Books.® These are representative listings only. They are by no means complete. These listings are to serve as a helpful guide to current market prices only.

684 *All Star Comic Paint Book.* Different authors and artists, contains drawings from popular comic strips, 3¾ x 8½ inches, 336 pages, considered a Big Little Paint Book,® very scarce in better condition, 1934.   **$15 $30 $45**

6825 *Big Big Paint Book, The.* 8½ x 11½ inches, 288 pages, sc, considered a Big Big Book,® 1936.   **$8 $15 $20**

nn *Captain Midnight's Trick and Riddle Book.* Similar to Penny Books,® others (?), scarce, 1930s.
$12 $18 $25

1018 *Fun Book, The.* FA (Fast Action®) type BLB, others in the series (?), very scarce, 1930s.
$10 $15 $22

? *One Hundred Best Known Fairy Tales.* Similar to the Big Little Nickel Books,® 1930s.
$4 $7 $11

713 *Stories from Shakespeare.* A Little Giant Book, Whitman (?), 1930s.
$5 $8 $13

Mystery and Adventure Series® Hardbacks (2300)

These books, also known as Adventure and Mystery Series,® were standard-sized hardbacks of approximately 250 pages and published by Whitman in the 1940s. They originally sold at dime stores for thirty-nine cents each. Reprint editions are numerous, but apparently this doesn't affect market prices. This is probably because there is some confusion as to which books are reprints and which are originals. Each title has appeared on various colored covers. For instance, the cover (under the dust jacket) of one book could be brown in one edition and green, blue, or tan in another. As to which color cover represented the first printing, it is hard to say. Most likely, the brown and green covers were the earliest editions as they are found almost exclusively on the books dated earlier. In addition to cover differences, some editions will have one listing of other books in the series (these listings are found in the back pages of the book), while another edition of the same book will have a different listing with books in the Fighters for Freedom Series.® The 2300 series is presented here because these books are about BLB characters, for the most part, and were written and illustrated by Whitman's BLB staff. Most of the movie star titles were written by Kathryn Heisenfelt. Prices here are for books with dust jackets. Those without dust jackets bring about 50 percent less.

? *Ann Rutherford and the Key to Nightmare Hall.* 1940s.
$4 $8 $11

? *Ann Sheridan and the Sign of the Sphinx.* 1940s.
$4 $8 $11

? *April Kane and the Dragon Lady, A Terry and the Pirates Adventure.* 1940s.
$5 $8 $12

? *Betty Grable and the House with the Iron Shutters.* 1940s.
$4 $8 $11

? *Betty Hutton and the Romance of Palmetto Island.* 1940s.
$4 $8 $11

? *Blondie and Dagwood's Adventure in Magic.* Chic Young, art adapted from comic strip, 1940s.
$5 $9 $13

? *Blondie and Dagwood's Secret Service.* Chic Young, art adapted from comic strip, 1940s.
$5 $9 $13

2388 *Blondie and Dagwood's Snapshot Clue.* Chic Young, art adapted from comic strip, 1943.
$5 $9 $13

2313 *Blue Streak and Doctor Medusa.* Art Elder, Francis Kirn art, 1946.
$4 $8 $11

? *Bonita Granville and the Mystery of Star Island.* 1940s.
$4 $8 $11

2331 *Boy Fighter with Andrew Jackson, A.* H.C. Thomas, Henry E. Vallely art, 1946.
$4 $8 $11

2314 *Boy Sailor with John Paul Jones, A.* H.C. Thomas, Henry E. Vallely art, 1946.
$4 $8 $11

? *Brenda Starr, Girl Reporter.* Dale Messick, 1940s.
$5 $9 $13

2355 *Deanna Durbin and the Adventure of Blue Valley.* Kathryn Heisenfelt, Hedwig Jo Meixner art, 1941.
$4 $8 $11

? *Deanna Durbin and the Feather of Flame.* 1940s.
$4 $8 $11

2331 *Dick Tracy, Ace Detective.* Chester Gould, 1943.
$5 $9 $13

? *Dick Tracy Meets the Night Crawler.* Chester Gould, 1940s.
$5 $9 $13

? *Don Winslow and the F.B.I.* Frank V. Martinek, 1940s.
$5 $8 $12

2327 *Don Winslow and the Scorpion's Stronghold.* Frank V. Martinek, Erwin L. Hess art, 1946.
$5 $8 $12

? *Gene Autry and the Golden Ladder Gang.* 1940s.
$4 $8 $12

2326 *Gene Autry and the Redwood Pirates.* Bob Hamilton, Erwin L. Hess art, 1946.
$4 $8 $12

? *Gene Autry and the Thief River Outlaws.* 1940s.
$4 $8 $12

? *Ginger Rogers and the Riddle of the Scarlet Cloak.* 1940s.
$4 $8 $11

? *Gregory Peck.* Complete title not known, Kathryn Heisenfelt, Henry E. Vallely art, very scarce, not listed in many back pages, if at all, 1940s.
$5 $9 $13

? *Invisible Scarlet O'Neil.* 1940s.
$4 $8 $12

? *Jane Withers and the Hidden Room.* 1940s.
$4 $8 $11

? *Jane Withers and the Phantom Violin.* 1940s.
$4 $8 $11

2301 *Jane Withers and the Swamp Wizard.* Kathryn Heisenfelt, Henry E. Vallely art, 1944.
$4 $8 $11

? *John Payne and the Menace at Hawk's Nest.* 1940s.
$4 $8 $11

2376 *Joyce of the Secret Squadron, A Captain Midnight Adventure.* R.R. Winterbotham, Erwin L. Darwin (really Erwin L. Hess) art, based on Captain Midnight radio series with Joyce Ryan, 1942.
$5 $9 $13

? *Judy Garland and the Hoodoo Costume.* 1940s.
$4 $8 $12

? *King of the Royal Mounted and the Ghost Guns of Roaring River.* 1940s.
$5 $8 $12

? *Little Orphan Annie and the Gila Monster Gang.* Harold Gray, 1940s.
$5 $9 $13

2317 *Long Rider and the Treasure of Vanished Men, The.* Gaylord DuBois, Henry E. Vallely art, 1946.
$4 $8 $11

? *Nina and Skeezix (of Gasoline Alley), The Problem of the Lost Ring.* Frank King, 1940s.
$5 $8 $12

? *Patty O'Neal, On the Airways.* 1940s.
$4 $8 $11

? *Peggy Parker, Girl Inventor.* 1940s.
$4 $8 $11

2330 *Phantom, The Son of the.* Dale Robertson sty, art from Lee Falk and Ray Moore's comic strip, origin of the Phantom, 1946.
$5 $9 $13

? *Polly the Powers Model, The Puzzle of the Haunted Camera.* 1940s.
$4 $8 $11

? *Quiz Kids and the Crazy Question Mystery.* 1940s.
$4 $8 $11

? *Red Ryder and the Adventure at Chimney Rock.* Fred Harman, 1940s.
$5 $8 $12

? *Red Ryder and the Mystery of the Whispering Walls*. Fred Harman, 1940s.
$5 $8 $12

? *Red Ryder and the Secret of Wolf Canyon*. Fred Harman, 1940s.
$5 $8 $12

? *Roy Rogers and the Ghost of Mystery Ranch*. 1940s.
$4 $8 $12

? *Roy Rogers and the Gopher Creek Gunman*. 1940s.
$4 $8 $12

? *Roy Rogers and the Outlaws of Sundown Valley*. 1940s.
$4 $8 $12

? *Roy Rogers and the Raiders of Sawtooth Ridge*. 1940s.
$4 $8 $12

? *Sandra of the Girl Orchestra*. 1940s.
$4 $8 $11

? *Shirley Temple and the Spirit of Dragonwood*. 1940s.
$5 $9 $13

? *Smilin' Jack and the Daredevil Girl Pilot*. Zack Mosley, 1940s.
$5 $9 $13

? *Sylvia Sanders and the Tangled Web*. 1940s.
$4 $8 $11

2384 *Tillie the Toiler and the Masquerading Duchess*. Russ Westover, art adapted from comic strip, 1943.
$5 $8 $12

? *Tom Harmon and the Great Gridiron Plot*. 1940s.
$4 $8 $11

? *Winnie Winkle and the Diamond Heirlooms*. 1940s.
$4 $8 $12

NBC Radio Script Plays® (Dick Tracy)

These books come in two volumes. Each is sixty-four pages long and measures 3¾ x 4 inches.

Vol. I *Dick Tracy and the Invisible Man*. Chester Gould art, 1939.
$12 $20 $30

Vol. II *Dick Tracy and the Ghost Ship*. Chester Gould art, 1939.
$12 $20 $30

Pop-up Books

This listing represents a variety of publishers and is incomplete. Use this for general reference only.

nn *Buck Rogers' Strange Adventures in the Spider Ship*. Phil Nowlan and Dick Calkins, scarce, 1935.
$35 $65 $110

nn *Dick Tracy, Capture of the Boris Arson Gang*. Chester Gould, 1935.
$30 $58 $100

nn *Mickey Mouse*. Walt Disney, Blue Ribbon Books, 1932.
$40 $85 $125

nn *Minnie Mouse*. Walt Disney, Blue Ribbon Books, 1932.
$35 $65 $110

? *Terry and the Pirates*. Milton Caniff, 1930s.
$25 $50 $85

? *Tim Tyler in the Jungle*. Lyman Young, 1935.
$25 $50 $85

Walt Disney Hardbound Series®

The Walt Disney hardbound books commonly considered Big Little Books® fall into three series: 845, 1058, and 1066. These three series are considered BLBs because they follow the traditional BLB format (one page of text opposite a drawing).

The 845 Series. Exact specifications of the 845 series are not known at the time of this printing.

nn *Donald Duck and His Cat Troubles.* 1947.
$10 $15 $22

nn *Mickey Mouse the Miracle Worker.* 1947.
$10 $15 $22

nn *Minnie Mouse and the Antique Chair.* 1947.
$10 $15 $22

nn *Poor Pluto.* 1947.
$9 $14 $19

The 1058 Series. This series is based on several Walt Disney cartoons. All books are 64 pages long and measure 4¾ x 5½ inches.

nn *Brave Little Tailor, The (with Mickey Mouse).* 1938.
$7 $12 $15

nn *Farmyard Symphony.* 1938.
$7 $11 $14

nn *Mother Pluto.* 1938.
$7 $12 $15

nn *Practical Pig, The.* 1938.
$7 $11 $14

nn *Timid Elmer.* 1938.
$7 $11 $14

nn *Ugly Duckling, The.* 1938.
$7 $12 $15

The 1066 Series. The books in this series measure 4¾ x 5½ inches and are 96 pages long.

nn *Clarabelle Cow, The Story of.* 1938.
$7 $11 $14

nn *Dippy the Goof, Walt Disney's Story of.* Later became Goofy during the story, tried both names in the same book, 1938.
$7 $12 $15

nn *Donald Duck, The Story of.* 1938.
$7 $12 $15

nn *Mickey Mouse, The Story of.* 1938.
$7 $12 $15

nn *Minnie Mouse, The Story of.* 1938.
$7 $12 $15

nn *Pluto the Pup, The Story of.* 1938.
$7 $12 $15

Saalfield Publishing Company

Saalfield Publishing Company
Akron, Ohio

In 1934, the Saalfield Publishing Company, famous for its many children's books and paper doll books, decided to get in on the Big Little Book® market. Their series of books, originally called Little Big Books,® began as long, horizontal books and were changed to a variety of sizes before settling on a standard size of 400 pages and 3½ x 4½ inches. Most of the Little Big Books® through early 1937 appear in two forms: hardcover editions (the 1000 and 1100 series) and soft-cover editions (the 1300, 1500, and 1600 series), which have the same covers and content as the hardcover editions. The hardcovers sold for fifteen cents and the soft-covers sold for ten cents. Since fewer soft-cover editions were purchased, and because of their inherently fragile nature, the soft-cover books bring an average of 30 percent more than hardcovers. During 1935 Saalfield published two numerically variant Little Big Books®: 283 and 284. These books, the *Pocket Coloring Book* and *The Midget Jumbo Coloring Book,* have become two of the most sought after of Saalfield's line. Because they were coloring books, they are hard to find in fine to mint conditions. The latter book may have contributed to an eventual name change, for in 1938, Saalfield changed the name of their line to Jumbo Books.®

Little Big Books® (1934-1938)

1138 *Bandits at Bay.* Charles T. Clinton, Paton Edwards art, 1938.
$5 $9 $11

1083 *Barney Google.* Bily DeBeck, odd-sized, 1935.
$10 $18 $25

1313 *Barney Google.* As above, except sc, 1935.
$14 $24 $34

1057 *Black Beauty.* Adapted from Anna Sewell, Park Sumner art, 1934.
$5 $9 $11

1307 *Black Beauty.* As above, except sc, 1934.
$7 $11 $15

1139 *Border Eagle, The.* Walker A. Thompkins, Joe Naef art, 1938.
$5 $9 $11

1059 *Brick Bradford and the City Beneath the Sea.* Clarence Gray and William Ritt, odd-sized, 1934.
$10 $20 $30

1309 *Brick Bradford and the City Beneath the Sea.* As above, except sc, 1934.
$15 $28 $40

1100 *Broadway Bill.* Mark Hellinger, Columbia movie with Myrna Loy and Warner Baxter, 1935.
$7 $11 $15

1580 *Broadway Bill.* As above, except sc, 1935.
$9 $14 $20

1135 *Buckskin and Bullets.* Ward M. Stevens, Luther Hittle art, 1938.
$5 $9 $11

1142 *Bullets Across the Border.* Guy Maynard, 1938.
$5 $9 $11

1091 *Burn 'Em Up Barnes.* Colbert Clark and John Rathmell sty, from Mascot movie with Frankie Darrow and Jack Mulhall, 1935.
$7 $11 $15

1321 *Burn 'Em Up Barnes.* As above, except sc, 1935.
$9 $14 $20

1107 *Camels Are Coming, The.* Tim Whelan and Russell Medcraft sty, from a Gaumont British Productions film with Jack Hulbert, 1935.
$9 $14 $20

1587 *Camels Are Coming, The.* As above, except sc, 1935.
$12 $19 $27

1093 *Chandu the Magician.* Harry Earnshaw and Vera Oldham sty, from Principal Pictures movie with Bela Lugosi, based on radio show, 1935.
$10 $18 $25

1323 *Chandu the Magician.* As above, except sc, 1935.
$14 $24 $34

1101 *Chief of the Rangers.* James Braden, from Mascot movie with Tom Mix, 1935.
$7 $11 $15

1581 *Chief of the Rangers.* As above, except sc, 1935.
$9 $14 $20

1127 *Corley of the Wilderness Trail.* Leonard K. Smith, Louis G. Schroeder art, 1937.
$5 $9 $11

1607 *Corley of the Wilderness Trail.* As above, except sc, 1937.
$7 $11 $15

1106 *Cowboy Millionaire, The.* Atherton Pictures movie with George O'Brien, 1935.
$7 $11 $15

1586 *Cowboy Millionaire, The.* As above, except sc, 1935.
$9 $14 $20

1136 *Desert Justice.* Ward M. Stevens, Park Sumner art, 1938.
$5 $9 $11

1114 *Dog Stars of Hollywood.* Gertrude Orr, photos of eighteen famous dogs, 1936.
$9 $14 $20

1594 *Dog Stars of Hollywood.* As above, except sc, 1936.
$12 $19 $27

1137 *Doomed to Die.* Charles T. Clinton, Paton Edwards art, 1938.
$7 $11 $15

1140 *Down Cartridge Creek.* Walker A. Tompkins, Henry Muheim art, 1938.
$5 $9 $11

1081 *Elmer and His Dog Spot.* Doc Winner, odd-sized, 1935.
$10 $18 $25

1311 *Elmer and His Dog Spot.* As above, except sc, 1935.
$14 $24 $34

1110 *Freddie Bartholomew, The Story of.* Helen Hoerle, photos from MGM movies, 1935.
$7 $11 $15

1590 *Freddie Bartholomew, The Story of.* As above, except sc, 1935.
$9 $14 $20

1097 *Go into Your Dance.* Bradford Ropes, from First National movie with Al Jolson and Ruby Keeler, 1935.
$7 $11 $15

1577 *Go into Your Dance.* As above, except sc, 1935.
$9 $14 $20

1111 *Hard Rock Harrigan (A Story of Boulder Dam).* Charles T. Clinton, from an Atherton Pictures movie with George O'Brien, 1935.
$7 $11 $15

1591 *Hard Rock Harrigan (A Story of Boulder Dam).* As above, except sc, 1935.
$9 $14 $20

1125 *Hockey Spare, The.* Harold M. Sherman, Robert A. Graef art, 1937.
$5 $9 $11

1605 *Hockey Spare, The.* As above, except sc, 1937.
$7 $11 $15

1098 *It Happened One Night.* Academy award-winning Columbia movie with Clark Gable and Claudette Colbert, 1935.
$10 $18 $25

1578 *It Happened One Night.* As above, except sc, 1935.
$14 $24 $34

1052 *Just Kids.* Ad Carter, horizontal Little Big Book,® 1934.
$12 $19 $27

1302 *Just Kids.* As above, except sc, not listed among Saalfield's files (does it exist?), 1934.
$20 $30 $40

1094 *Just Kids and the Mysterious Stranger.* Ad Carter, 1935.
$7 $11 $15

1324 *Just Kids and the Mysterious Stranger.* As above, except sc, 1935.
$9 $14 $20

1055 *Katzenjammer Kids in the Mountains.* H.H. Knerr, horizontal Little Big Book,® 1934.
$18 $25 $32

1305 *Katzenjammer Kids in the Mountains.* As above, except sc, 1934.
$24 $33 $41

1133 *Kelly King at Yale Hall.* Paschal Strong, Robert A. Graef art, 1937.
$5 $9 $11

1134 *King of Crime.* Joe Carson, Paton Edwards art, first standard-size Little Big Book,® 1938.
$7 $10 $14

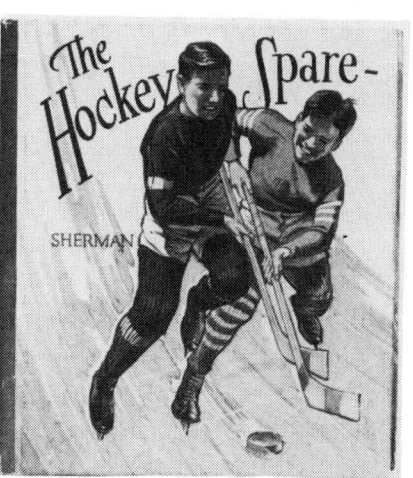

1105 *Kit Carson and the Mystery Riders.* Charles T. Clinton, from Mascot movie with Johnny Mack Brown and Noah Beery, 1935.
$7 $11 $15

1585 *Kit Carson and the Mystery Riders.* As above, except sc, 1935.
$9 $14 $20

1056 *Krazy Kat and Ignatz Mouse in Koko Land, Adventures of.* George Herriman, horizontal Little Big Book,® 1934.
$18 $25 $32

1306 *Krazy Kat and Ignatz Mouse in Koko Land, Adventures of.* As above, except sc, 1934.
$24 $33 $41

1128 *Last Man Out.* Harold Sherman, George Avison art, 1937.
$5 $9 $11

1086 *Laurel and Hardy.* Charles T. Clinton, scenes from five Hal Roach comedies, 1934.
$12 $19 $27

1316 *Laurel and Hardy.* As above, except sc, 1934.
$15 $24 $33

1092 *Law of the Wild, The.* Ford Beebe, Al Martin and John Rathmell sty, from Mascot Pictures movie with Rex, King of the Wild Horses, and Rin Tin Tin, Jr., 1935.
$7 $11 $15

1322 *Law of the Wild, The.* As above, except sc, 1935.
$9 $14 $20

1149 *Lee Brady, Range Detective.* Jack Chambers, Henry Muheim art, last Little Big Book® before name change to Jumbo Books,® 1938.
$7 $10 $14

1054 *Little Annie Rooney.* Brandon Walsh and Darrell McClure, horizontal Little Big Book,® 1934.
$14 $19 $25

1304 *Little Annie Rooney.* As above, except sc, 1934.
$18 $25 $32

1095   *Little Colonel, The.* Anne Fellows Johnston, from Twentieth Century-Fox movie with Shirley Temple and Lionel Barrymore, 1935.
$14 $19 $25

1575   *Little Colonel, The.* As above, except sc, 1935.
$18 $25 $32

1148   *Little Green Door, The.* Charles T. Clinton, Henry Muheim art, 1938.
$5 $9 $11

1112   *Little Hollywood Stars.* Dixie Wilson, photos of Spanky, Darla, Buckwheat, Alfalfa, Jackie Cooper, Mickey Rooney, 1935.
$10 $15 $22

1592   *Little Hollywood Stars.* As above, except sc, 1935.
$14 $19 $29

1087   *Little Jimmy's Gold Hunt.* Swinnerton, odd-sized, 1935.
$14 $19 $25

1317   *Little Jimmy's Gold Hunt.* As above, except sc, 1935.
$18 $25 $32

1118   *Little Lord Fauntleroy.* United Artists movie with Freddie Bartholomew, 1936.
$7 $10 $14

1598   *Little Lord Fauntleroy.* As above, except sc, 1936.
$9 $14 $17

1115   *Littlest Rebel, The.* Twentieth Century-Fox movie with Shirley Temple, 1935.
$14 $19 $25

1595   *Littlest Rebel, The.* As above, except sc, 1935.
$18 $25 $32

1103   *Lost Jungle, The (with Clyde Beatty).* Charles T. Clinton, Mascot movie, 1936.
$7 $11 $15

1583   *Lost Jungle, The (with Clyde Beatty).* As above, except sc, 1936.
$9 $14 $20

2113   *Midget Jumbo Coloring Book.* Number above is number on spine, different catalog number (284) found in Saalfield's files, very scarce in better condition, 1935.
$15 $40 $75

1116   *My Life and Times (Shirley Temple).* Max Trell, photos, 1936.
$14 $19 $25

1596   *My Life and Times (Shirley Temple).* As above, except sc, 1936.
$18 $25 $32

1146   *Nevada Rides the Danger Trail.* Jack Chambers, J.R. White, 1938.
$5 $9 $11

1147   *Nevada Whalen, Avenger.* Jack Chambers, Henry Muheim art, 1938.
$5 $9 $11

1099   *One Night of Love.* Charles Beahan and Dorothy Speare, from Columbia movie with Grace Moore, 1935.
$7 $11 $15

1579   *One Night of Love.* As above, except sc, 1935.
$9 $14 $20

1085   *Our Gang.* Charles T. Clinton, from Hal Roach movies, 1934.
$7 $11 $15

1315   *Our Gang.* As above, except sc, 1934.
$9 $14 $20

1084   *Peck's Bad Boy (Jackie Cooper in).* Charles T. Clinton, Twentieth Century-Fox movie, 1934.
$7 $11 $15

1314   *Peck's Bad Boy.* As above, except sc, 1934.
$9 $14 $20

1143   *Peril Afloat.* George Harmon Coxe, Eugene Paul art, 1938.
$7 $10 $14

1082   *Pete the Tramp, The Adventures of.* C.D. Russell, odd-sized, 1935.
$10 $18 $25

137

1312 *Pete the Tramp, The Adventures of.* As above, except sc, 1935.
$14 $24 $34

1130 *Phil Burton, Sleuth.* Leonard K. Smith, 1937.
$5 $9 $11

283 *Pocket Coloring Book.* Number here may be the publisher's catalog number only, book may have a different number on spine (see also *The Midget Jumbo Coloring Book*), scarce in better condition, 1935.
$15 $25 $45

1060 *Polly and Her Pals on the Farm.* Cliff Sterrett, comic strip is avidly sought, odd-sized, 1934.
$10 $18 $25

1310 *Polly and Her Pals on the Farm.* As above, except sc, 1934.
$14 $24 $34

1051 *Popeye.* Elzie Crisler Segar, first Little Big Book® published, horizontal, 1934.
$15 $25 $40

1301 *Popeye.* As above, except sc, not listed among the publisher's catalogs, most recent copy surfaced in 1981, rare, 1934.
$30 $60 $90

1088 *Popeye in Puddleburg.* Elzie Crisler Segar, 1934.
$12 $20 $30

1318 *Popeye in Puddleburg.* As above, except sc, 1934.
$16 $27 $40

1113 *Popeye Starring in Choose Your Weppins.* Adapted from a Max Fleischer cartoon by Charles T. Clinton, 1936.
$12 $20 $30

1593 *Popeye Starring in Choose Your Weppins.* As above, except sc, 1936.
$16 $27 $40

1117 *Popeye's Ark.* Elzie Crisler Segar, 1936.
$12 $20 $30

1597 *Popeye's Ark.* As above, except sc, 1936.
$16 $27 $40

1145 *Red-Hot Holsters.* Walker A. Tompkins, Henry Muheim art, 1938.
$5 $9 $11

1141 *Rio Raiders.* Guy Maynard, Albert H. Wick art, 1938.
$5 $9 $11

1089 *Shirley Temple, The Story of.* Grace Mack, from Twentieth Century-Fox and Paramount Pictures, 1934.
$10 $18 $25

1319 *Shirley Temple, The Story of.* As above, except sc, 1934.
$14 $24 $34

1144 *Spook Riders on the Overland.* Ward M. Stevens, W.A. Chase art, 1938.
$7 $10 $14

1132 *Stan Kent, Captain.* William Heyliger, Louis G. Schroeder art, 1937.
$5 $9 $11

1120 *Stan Kent, Freshman Fullback.* William Heyliger, Robert A. Graef art, 1936.
$5 $9 $11

1600 *Stan Kent, Freshman Fullback.* As above, except sc, 1936.
$7 $11 $15

1123 *Stan Kent, Varsity Man.* William Heyliger, Louis G. Schroeder art, 1936.
$5 $9 $11

1603 *Stan Kent, Varsity Man.* As above, except sc, 1936.
$7 $11 $15

1104 *Steel Arena, The (with Clyde Beatty).* Charles T. Clinton, from Mascot movie *The Lost Jungle*, see also Little Big Book 1103, *The Lost Jungle*, 1936.
$7 $11 $15

1584 *Steel Arena, The (with Clyde Beatty).* As above, except sc, 1936.
$9 $14 $20

1090 *Strawberry Roan.* Grace Mack, Universal movie with Ken Maynard, 1934. $7 $11 $15

1320 *Strawberry Roan.* As above, except sc, 1934.
$9 $14 $20

1129 *Three Finger Joe.* William Sherman, Robert A. Graef art, 1937.
$5 $9 $11

1108 *Tiger Lady, The (with Mabel Stark).* Gertrude Orr, photos of female lion tamer, 1935.
$7 $11 $15

1588 *Tiger Lady, The (with Mabel Stark).* As above, except sc, 1935.
$9 $14 $20

1053 *Tim Tyler.* Lyman Young, horizontal, 1934.
$15 $20 $28

1303 *Tim Tyler.* As above, except sc, 1934.
$20 $27 $37

1102 *Tom Mason on Top.* James A. Braden, Mascot movie with Tom Mix, 1935.
$9 $14 $20

1582 *Tom Mason on Top.* As above, except sc, 1935.
$12 $19 $27

1126 *Tommy of Troop Six.* Leonard K. Smith, Charles H. Towne art, 1937.
$5 $9 $11

1606 *Tommy of Troop Six.* As above, except sc, 1937.
$7 $11 $15

1058 *Tom Sawyer, The Adventures of.* From Mark Twain by Charles T. Clinton, Park Sumner art, 1934.
$12 $19 $27

1308 *Tom Sawyer, The Adventures of.* As above, except sc, 1934.
$15 $24 $33

1121 *West Pointers on the Gridiron.* Kennedy Lyons, Charles H. Towne art, 1936.
$5 $9 $11

1601 *West Pointers on the Gridiron.* As above, except sc, 1936.
$7 $11 $15

1124 *West Point Five.* Kennedy Lyons, George Avison art, 1937.
$5 $9 $11

1604 *West Point Five.* As above, except sc, 1937.
$7 $11 $15

1109 *We Three.* John Barrymore, MGM photos of Ethel, Lionel, and John Barrymore, 1935.
$9 $14 $20

1589 *We Three.* As above, except sc, 1935.
$12 $19 $27

1096 *Will Rogers, The Story of.* Jerome Beatty, Twentieth Century-Fox photos, 1935.
$9 $14 $20

1576 *Will Rogers, The Story of.* As above, except sc, 1935.
$12 $19 $27

1131 *Winged Four, The.* Kennedy Lyons, Louis G. Schroeder art, 1937.
$5 $9 $11

1122 *Winning Point, The.* Harold M. Sherman, George Avison art, 1936.
$5 $9 $11

1602 *Winning Point, The.* As above, except sc, 1936.
$7 $11 $15

Jumbo Books® (1938-1940)

The term Jumbo Book® never appeared on the Saalfield books, but was used for catalog reference by the publisher.

1175 *Abbie an' Slats.* Raeburn Van Buren, 1940.
$8 $13 $18

1182 *Abbie an' Slats and Becky.* Raeburn Van Buren, 1940.
$8 $13 $18

1178 *Billy of Bar-Zero.* Robert Marshall, Henry Muheim art, 1940.
$5 $9 $11

1159 *Billy the Kid on Tall Butte.* Robert Marshall, Joe Naef art, 1939.
$5 $9 $11

1174 *Billy the Kid's Pledge.* Robert Marshall, Neil Slocum art, 1940.
$5 $9 $11

1153 *Boss of the Chisholm Trail.* Guy L. Maynard, Ralph C. Hitchcock art, 1939.
$5 $9 $11

1181 *Broncho Bill.* Harry F. O'Neill, 1940.
$7 $10 $14

1169 *Bullet Benton.* J.W. McGuire, John Welch, 1939.
$5 $9 $11

1171 *Cowboy Malloy.* Mark Millis, Albert H. Wick art, 1940.
$5 $9 $11

1161 *Crimson Cloak, The.* Cleve Endicott, Henry Muheim art, 1939.
$7 $10 $14

1177 *Danger Trail North.* Jack Chambers, J.R. White, 1940.
$5 $9 $11

1160 *Dan of the Lazy L.* Mark Millis, Ralph C. Hitchcock art, 1939.
$5 $9 $11

1151 *Death by Short Wave.* Dick Adair, J.R. White art, 1938.
$7 $10 $14

1156 *Denny the Ace Detective.* Dick Adair, Henry Muheim art, 1938.
$7 $10 $14

1167 *Dixie Dugan Among the Cowboys.* J.P. McEvoy, John Streibel art, 1939.
$7 $11 $15

1188 *Dixie Dugan and Cuddles.* J.P. McEvoy, John Streibel art, 1940.
$7 $11 $15

1176 *Gentleman Joe Palooka.* Ham Fisher, 1940.
$8 $13 $18

1162 *G-Man Allen.* James McNeal, J.R. White art, 1939.
$6 $9 $12

1173 *G-Man in Action, A.* Dick Adair, J.R. White art, 1940.
$6 $9 $12

1157 *G-Men on the Trail.* James McNeal, J.R. White art, 1938.
$6 $9 $12

1172 *Gulliver's Travels.* Charles C. Taylor, based on Max Fleischer cartoon, 1939.
$7 $11 $15

1194 *Inspector Wade and the Feathered Serpent.* From Edgar Wallace, last Jumbo Book,® scarce, 1940.
$12 $19 $27

1186 *Inspector Wade of Scotland Yard.* From Edgar Wallace, 1940.
$9 $14 $20

1180 *Jim Hardy, Ace Reporter.* Dick Moores sty and art, 1940.
$6 $9 $12

1168 *Joe Palooka's Great Adventure.* Ham Fisher, 1939.
$8 $13 $18

1164 *Johnny Forty-Five.* Andrew A. Griffin, J.R. White, 1939.
$5 $9 $11

1184 *Just Kids and Deep-Sea Dan.* Ad Carter, 1940.
$7 $11 $15

1193 *Li'l Abner and Sadie Hawkins Day.* Al Capp, 1940.
$9 $14 $20

1187 *Li'l Abner and the Ratfields.* Al Capp, 1940.
$9 $14 $20

1192 *Little Mary Mixup and the Grocery Robberies.* R.M. Brinkerhoff, 1940.
$7 $11 $15

1190 *Major Hoople and His Horse (Our Boarding House).* 1940.
$7 $11 $15

1165 *Masked Man of the Mesa, The.* Cleve Endicott, Henry Muheim art, 1939.
$6 $9 $12

1170 *Mickey Finn.* Lank Leonard, 1940.
$8 $13 $18

1150 *Napoleon and Uncle Elby.* Clifford McBride, first Jumbo Book,® 1938.
$9 $14 $20

1166 *Napoleon, Uncle Elby and Little Mary.* Clifford McBride, 1939.
$8 $13 $18

1179 *Ned Brant, Adventure-Bound.* Bob Zuppke, 1940.
$5 $9 $11

1155 *$1000 Reward.* James McNeal, Henry Muheim art, ethnic stereotype, 1938.
$8 $13 $18

1163 *Ranger and the Cowboy, The.* Ward M. Stevens, Albert Wick art, 1939.
$5 $9 $11

1154 *Rangers on the Rio Grande.* Mark Millis, J.R. White art, 1938.
$5 $9 $11

1191 *Secret Agent K-7.* Gene Stafford, 1940.
$6 $9 $12

1152 *Son of Mystery.* Mark Millis, Henry Muheim art, 1939.
$6 $9 $12

1183 *Tailspin Tommy, Air Racer.* Hal Forrest, 1940.
$12 $19 $27

1158 *Tracked by a G-Man.* Dick Adair, Park Sumner art, 1939.
$6 $9 $12

1185 *Trail to Squaw Gulch, The.* Cleve Endicott, Lloyd Weidner art, 1940.
$5 $9 $11

1189 *Up Dead Horse Canyon.* Austin Gridley, Thomas Owings art, catalog title is *Up Dead Horse Canyon,* 1940.
$6 $9 $12

Dean and Son, Ltd. London, England

While this book deals primarily with BLBs produced in the United States, those made by Dean and Son are included because they are considered BLBs by some collectors. Big Little Books® or other similar books from non-English speaking countries are not included. The list below is incomplete. Dean and Son used the logo Great Big Midget Book.® The books measure 4 x 4½ inches and are 320 pages long. Publication dates are unknown.

nn *Bonzo Midget Book*
$2 $4 $6

nn *Bobby Bear's Midget Book*
$2 $4 $6

nn *Louis Wain's Midget Book*
$2 $4 $6

nn *Mickey Mouse Midget Book*
$5 $10 $15

Engel-Van Wiseman, Inc.
New York, New York

The Engel-Van Wiseman Corporation started making BLBs under the trademark Five Star Library.® Most of the twenty-three titles they produced were based on motion pictures. The books measure 4 x 5½ inches and have 158 pages.

1 *Count of Monte Cristo, The.* Adapted from Alexandre Dumas, Reliance Pictures with Robert Donat, 1934.
$12 $18 $25

13 *Dinky.* Helen M. Davidson, from Warner Brothers movie with Jackie Cooper, 1935.
$12 $18 $25

16 *Dog of Flanders, A.* Adapted from Ouida, RKO Pictures with Frankie Thomas, 1935.
$12 $18 $25

6 *Fighting President, The.* Jerome Van Wiseman and Wallace West, includes FDR's inaugural address, Universal Pictures feature film with Franklin D. Roosevelt, 1934.
$10 $15 $20

22 *Flaming Guns.* Book is advertised among some listings (does it exist?), 1935.
$17 $25 $35

8 *Great Expectations.* Adapted from Charles Dickens by A.J. Sharick, based on the Universal Pictures screenplay by Gladys Unger, with Henry Hull and Alan Hale, 1934.
$15 $22 $30

17 *Hoosier Schoolmaster, The.* Edward Finney, from Monogram Pictures with Norman Foster and Charlotte Henry, 1935.
$12 $18 $25

9 *Little Minister, The.* James M. Barrie, RKO Pictures with Katherine Hepburn and Alan Hale, 1935.
$12 $18 $25

19 *Lost City, The*. Charles Reed Jones, based on the movie serial with Bill Boyd, 1935.
$15 $22 $30

21 *Midsummer Night's Dream*. Helen Davidson, from Warner Brothers movie with Mickey Rooney, 1935.
$12 $18 $25

11 *Oliver Twist*. Adapted from Charles Dickens, Monogram Pictures with Dickie Moore, 1935.
$15 $22 $30

20 *Red Davis, The American Boy*. Adapted from Elaine Stearne Carrington's radio show, 1935.
$10 $15 $20

3 *Red Rider, The*. Harry Ormiston, Universal Pictures with Buck Jones, 1934.
$12 $18 $25

4 *Rider of Death Valley, The*. A.J. Sharick, from Universal Pictures with Tom Mix, 1934.
$15 $22 $30

10 *Robin Hood*. Austin Gilmore and Alex Gottlieb, from United Artists picture with Douglas Fairbanks, Sr., 1935.
$15 $22 $30

15 *Rocky Rhodes*. Harry Ormiston, from Universal Pictures with Buck Jones, 1935.
$12 $18 $25

14 *Speedwings*. Pat Patterson, from Columbia Pictures with Tim McCoy, 1935.
$14 $20 $28

12 *Stampede (Rex, King of the Wild Horses in)*. George Gerry, from Columbia Pictures, 1935.
$12 $18 $25

7 *Texas Bad Man*. A.J. Sharick, from Universal Pictures with Tom Mix, 1934.
$15 $22 $30

2 *Tim McCoy Beyond the Law*. Pat Patterson, from Columbia movie with Tim McCoy, 1934.
$12 $18 $25

18 *Westward Ho!* Edward Finney, from Republic Pictures with John Wayne, 1935.
$20 $30 $40

5 *Wheels of Destiny*. Harry Ormiston, from Universal Pictures with Ken Maynard, 1934.
$12 $18 $25

23 *World of Monsters, The*. From movie with Frank Sage, advertised among some listings (does it exist?), see also *Flaming Guns*, 1935.
$17 $25 $35

Fawcett Publications, Inc.
Greenwich, Connecticut

In 1941, Fawcett Publications produced four titles under their Dime Action® novel series. These books were nearly identical to the Dell Fast Action® BLBs. The Dime Actions® are 192 pages long and measure 4 x 5½ inches. The inside covers advertise various Fawcett comic books, including *Master Comics* and *Whiz Comics*, sources for the Dime Action® stories.

nn *Bulletman and Bulletgirl.* 1941.
$17 $25 $35

nn *Captain Marvel and the Return of the Scorpion.* Bill Parker, C.C. Beck art, 1941.
$20 $30 $40

nn *Minute Man, the One Man Army (and the Mystery of the Spy Ring).* 1941.
$17 $25 $35

nn *Spy Smasher and the Red Death.* 1941.
$17 $25 $35

Golden Press Publishing Company (Western Publishing) Racine, Wisconsin

Released in the United States in 1967, the Golden Star Books® were originally published in Paris, France, in 1966 under the publishing name Deux Coqs d'Or. These books are very similar to the A Big Little Book® Series books, which were also published by Western in the 1960s (under the name Whitman Publishing). The Golden Star Books® contain color and black and white illustrations and are 248 pages long.

? *Adventure Tales.* Kathryn and Byron Jackson, Gustaf Tenggren art, 1967.
$2 $3 $6

? *Animal Tales.* Georges Duplaix, Feodor Rojankovsky art, 1967.
$2 $3 $6

6080 *Animals of the Little Wood.* A.M. Dalmais, Paul Durand art, 1967.
$2 $3 $6

? *Autumn Tales.* Kathryn Jackson, Richard Scarry art, 1967.
$2 $3 $6

? *Henry Rabbit, The Adventures of.* A.M. Duplaix, Paul Durand art, 1967.
$2 $3 $6

? *Little Tiger, The Adventures of.* Kathleen Daly, J.P. Miller art, 1967.
$2 $3 $6

? *Peter Pan, Walt Disney's.* Walt Disney Studios, 1967.
$3 $5 $9

? *Pinocchio, Walt Disney's.* Walt Disney Studios, 1967.
$3 $5 $9

?	*Sleeping Beauty, Walt Disney's.* Walt Disney Studios, 1967.			
		$3	$5	$9
?	*Snow White, Walt Disney's.* Walt Disney Studios, 1967.			
		$3	$5	$9
?	*Springtime Tales.* Kathryn Jackson, Richard Scarry art, 1967.			
		$2	$3	$6
6079	*Winter Tales.* Kathryn Jackson, Richard Scarry art, 1967.			
		$2	$3	$6

Goldsmith Publishing Company Chicago, Illinois

From 1934 to 1935, the Goldsmith Publishing Company produced four titles in their Radio Star Series.® Goldsmith's most commendable contribution was the introduction of artist Henry E. Vallely to the Big Little Book® field. Vallely went on to Whitman to produce some of the more respectable BLBs.

nn *Eddie Cantor in Laughland.* Harold Sherman, Henry E. Vallely art, 1934.
$14 $20 $27

nn *Fire Chief Ed Wynn and His Old Fire Horse.* Harold Sherman, Henry E. Vallely art, 1934.
$14 $20 $27

nn *Jack Pearl as Detective Baron Munchausen.* Harold Sherman, Henry E. Vallely art, 1934.
$14 $20 $27

nn *Joe Penner's Duck Farm.* Harold Sherman, Henry E. Vallely art, 1935.
$14 $20 $27

Lynn Publishing Company, Inc. New York, New York

In 1935, the Lynn Publishing Company began the A Lynn Book® Series. The exact number of titles published is not yet known, and many gaps in numbering exist. There are three distinct forms of Lynn Books®: (1) 4 x 6 inches, 192 pages with standard BLB format (alternating pictures with text); (2) 5 x 7 inches, 128 pages long with standard BLB format; and (3) 5 x 7 inches, 94 pages long with a four-color picture on every page. The series ended in 1936.

L21 *Blondie and Dagwood.* Chic Young, 5 x 7 inches, 94 pages, four-color illustration, 1936.
$20 $30 $40

L11 *Call of the Wild (Jack London's).* Rex Carson, from Twentieth Century-Fox movie with Clark Gable, 1935.
$15 $22 $30

L20 *Ceiling Zero.* From Warner Brothers movie with James Cagney and Pat O'Brien, 5 x 7 inches, 128 pages, 1935.
$15 $22 $30

L14 *Chip Collins' Adventures on Bat Island.* Gerald Breitigam, Jack Wilhelm art, 1935.
$12 $18 $25

L19 *Curley Harper at Lakespur.* Gerald Breitigam, Lyman Young art, 1935.
$12 $18 $25

L13 *Donnie and the Pirates.* George Gerry, Darrell McClure art, 1935.
$12 $18 $25

L24 *Dumb Dora and Bing Brown.* Gerald Breitigam, Bill Dwyer art, 5 x 7 inches, 94 pages, four-color illustration, 1936.
$17 $25 $35

L27 *Jimmy Allen in the Sky Parade.* Wallace West, from Paramount movie, 5 x 7 inches, 128 pages, 1936.
$15 $22 $30

L15 *Jimmy and the Tiger.* George Gerry, Vic Forsythe art, 1935.
$12 $18 $25

L30 *Last of the Mohicans, The.* Charles Reed Jones, from a United Artists movie with Randolph Scott, 4 x 6 inches, 192 pages, same format, size, and page count as the first ten books (L10 to L19), 1936.
$15 $22 $30

L10 *Les Miserables (Victor Hugo's).* Lewis Graham, from Twentieth Century-Fox movie with Fredric March and Charles Laughton, 1935.
$15 $22 $30

L17 *O'Shaughnessy's Boy.* L. Mitchell, from MGM movie with Jackie Cooper and Wallace Beery, 1935.
$12 $18 $25

L12 *Scrappy, The Adventures of.* Hal Hode, from Columbia Pictures cartoon, 1935.
$17 $25 $35

L16 *Tale of Two Cities (Charles Dickens').* Gerald Breitigam, from MGM movie with Ronald Colman, 1935.
$12 $18 $25

L26 *13 Hours by Air.* Wallace West, from Paramount Pictures with Fred MacMurray, 5 x 7 inches, 128 pages, 1936.
$17 $25 $35

L25 *Trail of the Lonesome Pine, The.* Wallace West, from Paramount movie with Henry Fonda and Fred MacMurray, 5 x 7 inches, 128 pages, 1936.
$20 $30 $40

L18 *Western Frontier.* George Gerry, Columbia Pictures with Ken Maynard, 1935.
$15 $22 $30

McLoughlin Brothers Publishing Company
Springfield, Massachusetts

In 1934, the McLoughlin Brothers Publishing Company began producing children's books using the series names Little Big Books® and Little Big Classics.® The list below is not complete, and is presented mainly because McLoughlin used the same name (Little Big Books®) as Saalfield. The McLoughlin books are larger than normal BLBs and are hardcover.

nn   *My ABC Book.* 1938.
                                    $2 $4 $6

nn   *My Book of Good Old Stories.* 1934.
                                    $2 $4 $6

nn   *Nature Stories for Tiny Folks.* 1930s.
                                    $2 $4 $6

nn   *Pinocchio.* 1938.
                                    $4 $7 $10

nn   *Treasure Island.* 1938.
                                    $3 $6 $9

nn   *Ugly Duckling, The.* 1939.
                                    $3 $5 $8

Ottenheimer Publishers, Inc.
Baltimore, Maryland

In 1977, Ottenheimer Publishers produced eight titles in BLB format based on the Hanna-Barbera Flintstones cartoons. All of these books have soft covers, are 240 pages long, and measure 3½ x 4½ inches. Each book was written by Horace J. Elias, with artwork adapted from Hanna-Barbera Studio Productions. A flip movie was added to every book. The books sold for 49 cents.

nn   *Flintstones, A Friend from the Past.* FM, 1977.
                                    under $1 $1

nn   *Flintstones, It's About Time.* FM, 1977.
                                    under $1 $1

nn   *Flintstones, Pebbles and Bamm-Bamm Meet Santa Claus.* FM, 1977.
                                    under $1 $1

nn   *Flintstones, The Great Balloon Race.* FM, 1977.
                                    under $1 $1

nn   *Flintstones, The Mystery of the Many Missing Things.* Taken and redrawn from Whitman's 2014 (1968), FM, 1977.
                                    under $1 $1

nn   *Huckleberry Hound, Newspaper Reporter.* FM, 1977.
                                    under $1 $1

4510 *Treasure Island.* Robert Louis Stevenson, A.J. McAllister art, 1977.
under $1.50 $2

4507 *20,000 Leagues Under the Sea.* Jules Verne, Pablo Marcos Studios art, 1977.
under $1.50 $2

4501 *Wizard of Oz, The.* L. Frank Baum, Pablo Marcos Studios art, 1977.
under $1.50 $2

nn *Yogi Bear Goes Country and Western.* FM, 1977.
under $1 $1

nn *Yogi Bear Saves Jellystone Park.* FM, 1977.
under $1 $1

4514 *Tom Sawyer, The Adventures of.* Mark Twain, Pablo Marcos Studios art, 1979.
under $1.50 $2

Playmore Incorporated
New York, New York

In 1977, Playmore Incorporated, under their imprint, Moby Illustrated Classics, published twelve soft-cover books using the BLB format. In 1979, twelve more books were produced. The company plans to continue publishing these types of books. Playmore is the Classics Illustrated (remember the comic books that were used as substitutes for the real thing?) of the BLB field. All of their stories come from the classics. The books measure 4⅛ x 5½ inches and are 240 pages long. In 1979, they sold for 95 cents. All cover pictures were painted by Al Lanier.

4512 *Around the World in Eighty Days.* Jules Verne, Pablo Marco Studios art, 1977.
under $1.50 $2

4504 *Black Beauty.* Anna Sewell, 1977.
under $1.50 $2

4515 *Call of the Wild, The.* Jack London, Pablo Marcos Studios art, 1979.
under $1.50 $2

4506 *Connecticut Yankee in King Arthur's Court, A.* Mark Twain, 1977.
under $1 $2

4519 *Count of Monte Cristo, The.* Alexandre Dumas, Pablo Marcos Studios art, 1979.
under $1 $2

4518 *David Copperfield.* Charles Dickens, Pablo Marcos Studios art, 1979.
under $1 $2

4508 *Heidi.* Johanna Spyri, 1977.
under $1 $2

4516 *Huckleberry Finn, The Adventures of.* Mark Twain, Craig Flessel art, 1979.
under $1 $2

4505 *Kidnapped.* Robert Louis Stevenson, 1977.
under $1 $2

4521 *Last of the Mohicans, The.* James Fenimore Cooper, 1979.
under $1 $2

4511 *Little Women.* Louisa May Alcott, Pablo Marcos Studios art, 1977.
under $1 $2

153

4520 *Moby Dick.* Herman Melville, Brendan Lynch art, 1979.
under $1 $2

4522 *Mutiny on Board H.M.S. Bounty, The.* Herman Melville, Brendan Lynch art, 1979.
under $1 $2

4517 *Oliver Twist.* Charles Dickens, art by comic book artist Ric Estrada, 1979.
under $1.25 $2

4523 *Oregon Trail, The.* Francis Parkman, Dave Simons, 1979.
under $1 $2

4513 *Robin Hood, The Merry Adventures of.* Howard Pyle, Pablo Marcos Studios art, 1979.
under $1 $2

4503 *Robinson Crusoe, The Adventures of.* Daniel Defoe, 1977.
under $1 $2

4502 *Sherlock Holmes and the Case of the Hound of the Baskervilles.* A. Conan Doyle, Pablo Marcos Studios art, 1977.
under $1.25 $2

4524 *Tales of Mystery and Terror.* Edgar Allan Poe, Pablo Marcos Studios art, 1979.
under $1 $2

4509 *Three Musketeers, The.* Alexandre Dumas, Pablo Marcos Studios art, 1977.
under $1 $2

Samuel Lowe Company
Kenosha, Wisconsin

In 1949, the Samuel Lowe Company published a set of ten Swap-It® Books featuring cowboy stories. Each book is hardcovered with red tape spines. They are thirty-two pages long and measure 3½ x 4¼ inches. They were published under a 582 series number, which appears on the back cover of each book along with a listing of other titles in the series. Some have blue back covers, while others have red. In addition to the ten regular issues, some softcover versions of the Swap-It® Books also exist under the name Smokey Joe of the Glendale Riders Series.® These books were made as giveaways for the Glendale Hot-Dog Company. Only four of these giveaways are known to exist, although there may be others. Since the artwork and stories for the giveaway books are identical to the hardcovered books, with the exception of a name change, there is a possibility that all ten books in the regular series had softcover, giveaway editions.

The Swap-It® Books

582 *Bud Shinners and the Oregon Trail.* Ben Bolt, Jack Crowe art, 1949.
$2 $5 $8

582 *Danny Meets the Cowboys.* Sam Edwards, Richard Osborne art, 1949.
$2 $5 $8

582 *Flint Adams and the Stage Coach.* Jim Daniels, Jack Crowe art, 1949.
　　　　　　　$2　$5　$8

582 *Get Them, Cowboy.* 1949.
　　　　　　　$2　$5　$8

582 *Little Tex Comes to XY Ranch.* 1949.
　　　　　　　$2　$5　$8

582 *Little Tex in the Midst of Trouble.* Ben Bolt, Jack Crowe art, 1949.
　　　　　　　$2　$5　$8

582 *Little Tex's Escape.* 1949.
　　　　　　　$2　$5　$8

582 *Mail Must Go Through, The (A Story of the Pony Express).* Alan James, Richard Osborne art, 1949.
　　　　　　　$2　$5　$8

582 *Nevada Jones, Trouble Shooter.* Joe Adams, Richard Osborne art, 1949.
　　　　　　　$2　$5　$8

582 *Outlaws' Last Ride, The.* Richard Osborne sty and art, 1949.
　　　　　　　$2　$5　$8

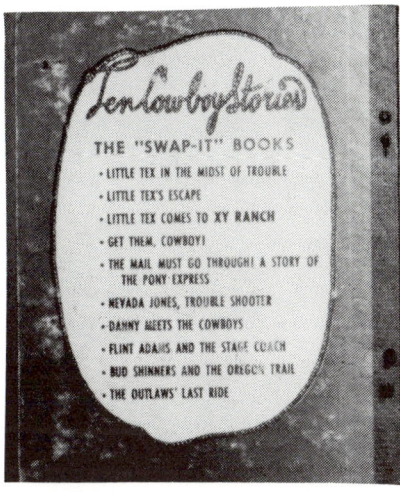

155

Smokey Joe of the Glendale Riders®

nn *Danny Meets the Cowboys.* Sam Edwards, Richard Osborne art, rare, 1949.
$12 $16 $22

nn *Little Tex Comes to XY Ranch.* Rare, 1949.
$12 $16 $22

nn *Outlaws' Last Ride, The.* Richard Osborne sty and art, rare, 1949.
$12 $16 $22

nn *Smokey Joe, Trouble Shooter.* Joe Adams, Richard Osborne art, name change from Nevada Jones, any other Smokey Joe titles would be worth the amount given for this one, rare, 1949.
$15 $19 $25

Wehrle, Joe, Jr.
Punxsutawney, Pennsylvania

Not really a corporation, Mr. Wehrle is an artist who, in 1981, produced the first book to follow the old BLB format since the 1940s. Using the series name Teacup Tales,® Mr. Wehrle presents the character, Cauliflower Catnip, in BLB form. His book has 280 pages and, I suppose, can still be purchased for $4.95 plus 50 cents postage from Joe Wehrle, Jr., P.O. Box 41, Punxsutawney, Pennsylvania 15767.

nn *Cauliflower Catnip, Pearls of Peril.* Joe Wehrle, Jr., signed and numbered edition with advance order, 1981.
$2 $4 $7

nn *Cauliflower Catnip, Pearls of Peril.* As above, except not signed or numbered, 1981.
$2 $4 $6

World Syndicate Publishing Company
Cleveland, Ohio and New York, New York

In 1933, the World Syndicate Publishing Company produced the first of their Highlights of History Series.® The books are based on a comic strip written and drawn by J. Carroll Mansfield. The books are all-picture, with text inside each drawing. Each book was printed with a different cover. All but *Pioneers of the Wild West* have both a regular illustrated hardcover and a cloth-bound version in a solid color. The differences in covers generally make no difference in price, with the exception of the above-mentioned book. The books measure 3¾ x 4¼ inches and are of various page lengths.

nn *Buffalo Bill.* J. Carroll Mansfield, illustrated, full-color cover, 1934.
$10 $15 $20

nn *Buffalo Bill.* As above, except blue cloth-bound, 1934.
$10 $15 $20

nn *Daniel Boone.* J. Carroll Mansfield, illustrated, full-color cover, 1934.
$10 $15 $20

nn *Daniel Boone.* As above, except blue cloth-bound, 1934.
$10 $15 $20

nn *Kit Carson.* J. Carroll Mansfield, illustrated, full-color cover, 1933.
$10 $15 $20

nn *Kit Carson.* As above, except black cloth-bound, 1933.
$10 $15 $20

nn *Pioneers of the Wild West.* J. Carroll Mansfield, blue cloth-bound edition, 1933.
$10 $15 $20

nn *Pioneers of the Wild West.* As above, except red cloth-bound, 1933.
$12 $18 $25

nn *Pioneers of the Wild West.* As above, except white cloth-bound, 1933.
      $15 $22 $30

nn *Pioneers of the Wild West.* As above, except black cloth-bound, 1933.
      $15 $22 $30

nn *Winning of the Old Northwest, The.* J. Carroll Mansfield, illustrated, full-color cover, 1934.
      $12 $18 $25

nn *Winning of the Old Northwest, The.* As above, except blue cloth-bound, 1934.
      $12 $18 $25

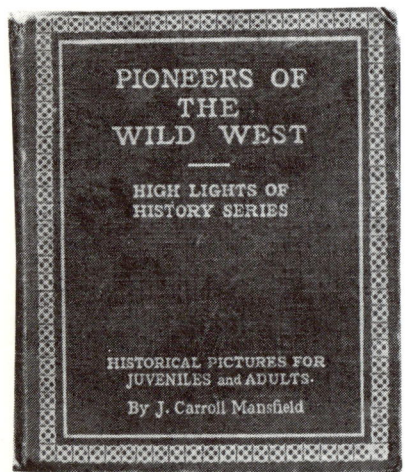

About the Author

Jim Thomas, twenty-two, is a Kentucky resident and a 1983 graduate of the Johns Hopkins University, receiving his degree in Political Science.

He is a freelance writer, cartoonist, a graphic artist and does some work in filmmaking. He began collecting antiques and nostalgia twelve years ago. Since then, he has extended his interests into nearly every form of collectible. His research for *The Big Little Book Price Guide* began more than three years ago and has been punctuated by the appearance of his articles on the publications in the comic-collecting field in a number of periodicals.

(The author would like to express his sincere appreciation to his friend, Henry Chen, who, among other things of greater importance, contributed the use of his tie in the above photograph. The author does not wish to acknowledge the photographer responsible.)